SCOTLAND
STREET
PRESS

HAIRAN

Published in 2024 by
Scotland Street Press, Edinburgh
scotlandstreetpress.com

A CIP record for this book is available from the British Library.

ISBN: 978-1-910895-96-2

Printed on responsibly sourced paper.

Book concept, design and layout: Daoud Sarhandi-Williams
Cover design and plaited hair graphic: Emily Benton
Typeset in Palatino Linotype, Avenir, and Maragsa

HAIRAN

**Poems of Hair and Freedom
by Iranian Women in Times
of Repression and Struggle**

Edited by
DAOUD SARHANDI-WILLIAMS
& ALI SOBATI

Translator
ALI SOBATI

Co-editors (alphabetically)
ABBAS SHOKRI
ANAHITA REZAEI
ANNA KRASNOWOLSKA
SEPIDEH JODEYRI
SEPIDEH KOUTI

Mahsa Amini's grave (see p.15).

Dedicated to

MAHSA (JÎNA) AMINI
20.07.2000–16.09.2022

and other Woman Life Freedom
activists killed or forced into exile
in the aftermath of her death.

CONTENTS

Poster by Najmeh Yazdanibakhsh.

EDITORS AND TRANSLATOR

DAOUD SARHANDI-WILLIAMS (Great Britain, 1962) is a multidisciplinary filmmaker and writer of Anglo-Indian and Pakistani heritage. In the 1980s and 90s he worked as a film editor in London and Northern Ireland. At BBC Elstree Studios he cut many films for the British documentary filmmaker, Paul Watson. Subsequently, he has worked as an independent researcher, writer, filmmaker, and photographer, principally in Bosnia, Mexico, Palestine, Ukraine, and Spain. His previous books include *Bosnian War Posters* and *Ukraine at War: Street Art, Posters + Poetry.* Since 2003, he has been a regular contributor to *Eye Magazine*, London. Award-winning documentary films produced by Sarhandi-Williams – alongside Carolina Rivas – include *The Colour of Olives* (Palestine, 2006), and *Lessons for Zafirah* (Mexico, 2011). Also with Ms Rivas, he produces the *Video Values* series of short films.

ALI SOBATI (Iran, 1981) has been a poet, critic, essayist, journalist, translator, and university lecturer in literature for over two decades. He has emerged as one of the most prominent Iranian academic literary voices of his generation. Sobati is widely recognised for his sociopolitical organisational role within the Iranian literary communities, both within his homeland and in the diaspora. At present, he resides outside of Iran – to where he feels it is unsafe to return due to his involvement in the Woman Life Freedom movement.

To me, freedom means not being afraid. Poster by Akef Rahmati.

CO-EDITORS (alphabetically)

ABBAS SHOKRI (Iran, 1955) fled Iran in 1989 to save his life, settling in Oslo, Norway. He founded Aftab, a Persian language press that publishes censored Iranian authors. In 1995, he retrained as a journalist – a profession he still works in. He is the author of fourteen poetry books.

ANAHITA REZAEI (Iran, 1971) is an award-winning writer and literary critic living in Tehran, Iran. Her previous works include *Silent and Quiet of Being – Not Being Days* and *The Shooting Right to Domestic Dogs.* Since 2020, she has been a member of the editorial board of *Poshtebam* fine arts magazine.

ANNA KRASNOWOLSKA (Poland, 1949) is a professor and specialist in Persian literature and Iranian culture. She was the director of the Institute of Oriental Studies (1999–2002) and the head of the Department of Iranian Studies (2000–17) at Jagiellonian University, Kraków, Poland.

SEPIDEH JODEYRI (Iran, 1976) is an award-winning poet and translator living in Washington, DC, USA. She is the author of eleven books, and was a selected poet of The Dangerous Women project at the University of Edinburgh. She worked with both Abbas Shokri and Ali Sobati in the development of this book.

SEPIDEH KOUTI (Iran, 1977) is a poet, author, translator, and editor. She began her literary career in 2000, authoring entries for the *Encyclopedia of Persian Literature* and the Academy of Persian Language and Literature. Previous works include *The Creeping Shadow of Objects* and *On the Heights of Despair* (as translator). Additionally, she practices as an emergency medicine specialist in Iran.

Poster by Rashid Rahnama.

NOTE ON THE ILLUSTRATIONS

The thirteen anonymous portraits in this anthology
were commissioned for this book, and provided by some
of the poets included. All were sent to the editors in low-
resolution and by messenger apps.

The political posters included in *Hairan* were created to
support the Woman Life Freedom movement. All are
by Iranian designers, and three (pp. 10, 16 and 22) are
by women. The editors are grateful to Hervé Matine at
4tomorrow Association, Paris, for sharing these images
with us.

The photograph on page six depicts Mahsa Amini's
grave in the cemetery of Aychi, Kurdistan province,
Iran. It is credited to "Derafsh", was taken in June
2023, and shared for public use on https://commons.
wikimedia.org. The photo has been cropped at the
bottom for this publication.

After Mahsa Amini was killed in police custody, the
graphic "code" shown on page seven appeared in Iran,
and began circulating among opponents of the regime.
It reveals the words "Woman Life Freedom", written in
Farsi, using the colours of the Iranian flag. The original
designer remains unknown. The poem *For You, The Code*
(p. 172) references this graphic in light of Amini's death.

All illustrations in *Hairan* have been converted to black-
and-white from their original colour copies.

Poster by Ghazal Hosseini.

PREFACE BY DAOUD SARHANDI-WILLIAMS

I was sitting at my desk in September 2022, working on a book featuring poetry written by citizens in war-torn Ukraine, when I heard the shocking news about a young Kurdish-Iranian woman called Mahsa Amini. She had been arrested in Tehran and killed in police custody for not covering her hair in the decreed way.

Throughout Iran, women and girls of all ages rose in fury against the regime. The mandatory hijab head covering, alongside hair itself, became a powerful symbol in a struggle for women's liberation, personal freedom, and choice.

In the autumn of 2022, I didn't know much about Iranian poetry. However, I decided to find out how contemporary female Iranian poets were responding to their oppression. This curiosity was undoubtedly raised by my work with Ukrainian war poetry, most of which was written by women living the day-to-day horrors of Russia's war against their country.

Shortly after becoming interested in Iranian poetry, I had an extraordinary stroke of good luck. My translator was coming to the end of her work on the Ukrainian poems, and one day I jokingly commented, "It's a pity you don't speak Farsi. I'd love to do something with Iranian poetry, and it'd be so nice to keep working together."

"I don't speak a word," she replied, "but my sister is a professor of Farsi. I can put you in touch." In this highly synchronous way, I got to know and work with Anna Krasnowolska, a respected Polish Iranologist. Anna had recently retired from her professorship at the Jagiellonian University in Kraków, and she was interested in helping me with my research.

In early January 2023, Anna suggested we reach out to Abbas Shokri, an Iranian publisher and author she knew well. Abbas, a resident of Oslo, Norway, then contacted established female poets in Iran and the Iranian diaspora, inviting them to submit poems for publication. At the end of February, he sent me more than two hundred pages of poetry from a large group of contemporary poets.

Abbas and Anna determined the initial selection from these poems,[1] and soon after, Anna chose and translated ten so that I – a non-Farsi speaker – could get an idea of the style and substance of the work we had been sent.

Ali Sobati is an Iranian Farsi-English translator and contemporary poetry critic living in Toronto, Canada. After Abbas introduced us, Ali and I collaborated closely for the rest of this project, with him tackling all the translations. I also invited him to supervise the final selection of poems, edit the book alongside me, and write the introduction.[2]

Before detailed literary work could get underway, however, Ali felt that the list of contributing poets was incomplete. So, we began working in close collaboration with three female Iranian poets – Sepideh Jodeyri (who, I discovered, had also helped Abbas at the inception of this project), Sepideh Kouti, and Anahita Rezaei, all of whom have poems in this anthology. Thus, a shortlist of important "missing" poets was drawn up; Ali and his female team then reached out to them by mail and messenger apps.

The three women named above were vitally important to the development of this book.[3] For this reason, Ali and I asked them to contribute to the introduction and be acknowledged as co-editors alongside Abbas and Anna.[4]

I became the editorial project manager and book designer. Right at the start of this project, I had encouraged Abbas to ask poets for photographs of their hair, half-thinking they might find my request outlandish. However, most of them responded positively.[5] Later, in Paris, I also discovered an archive of Iranian political posters from which a handful of images were selected.

In this way, an initially abstract idea evolved into a multinational team effort. Nonetheless, without the generous participation of the poets,[6] *Hairan* would have fallen at the first hurdle.[7] Moreover, it was brave of them to trust me, a complete unknown in the Iranian literary world, contacting them through people I had never met in person.[8]

As this book goes to press, well over two hundred Iranian protesters have died, thousands have been arrested, and unknown numbers have been tortured. Several male demonstrators have been executed, often after being convicted on trumped-up charges under a catch-all crime that translates into English as "corruption on earth". Furthermore, many Iranians have been forced to flee into exile, joining a diaspora that now numbers between four and eight million people.[9]

Despite ongoing protests, however, the Iranian regime seems to be doubling down on its efforts to restrict women's rights. Shops will be penalised if they serve a woman who enters their premises with her head uncovered, smart cameras that can spot women who aren't covering their hair "correctly" are being installed in urban spaces, and the "crime" of not wearing a hijab outdoors is being considered for a mandatory ten-year prison term – up from a maximum of two months. In all these ways, public spaces that are safe for dissenting women in Iran are shrinking and becoming more dangerous.

The objectives of this book are twofold: to share with the general reader an extraordinary collection of contemporary Iranian women's poetry that has rarely, if ever, been translated on this scale. The verse is passionate, inspiring, and hallucinatory in its mix of beauty and horror, courage and fear, despair and hope. Collectively, it powerfully expresses the sentiment that words – and *poetic* words – can still play a vital role in bringing about social and political change. It shows us that poetry *matters*.

The second objective of this book is to promote women's civil and human rights in Iran, as well as in other countries that adhere to similar or even more extreme doctrines regarding the role and place of women and girls. As this book goes to press, a resurgent Taliban in Afghanistan (a country to which I have historic family connections) has not only banned secondary and higher education for girls, but is also bringing back the public stoning of women judged "guilty" of some reported moral failing or petty misconduct. Meanwhile, arresting and then sexually abusing Afghan women for "bad hijab" is routine.[10]

Does the world need to stop turning before such barbaric misogyny ends?

Do conscientious journalists, protesters, and even poets have to run out of words before these regimes listen, learn, and change?

Let us hope not.

Instead, let us hope that Muslim women will have the freedom to cover or not cover their hair, and that both choices will be treated equally. And that such basic liberties will extend to all aspects of their lives.

---

[1] Many of the poems submitted to the editors were written for this anthology, while some poets contributed poems from their unpublished archives. Several poems may also have been previously self-published on personal blogs or websites.

[2] At various stages, the entire Farsi-speaking editorial team was involved in the selection process. I trusted this working method completely and only declined to include two poems that had been selected. Alternative poems by the same poets were then chosen.

[3] As the only native-English speaker on the team, I also worked hand-in-hand with Ali to polish the English translations and edit and supplement the footnotes to the poems and introduction.

[4] Each female poet/editor wrote one of the historical sections of the introduction. Ali Sobati then edited and translated these texts before adding his sections about Iranian contemporary poetry.

[5] Abbas Shokri – and later, Ali Sobati and the Iranian female editors – asked poets to send photos of their hair to accompany their poems. Many also sent images of their faces, but to protect the security of these women, I decided not to publish these.

[6] Although none of the editors counted how many poets included in this anthology live in Iran rather than in the diaspora, they calculated that the split is around half.

[7] "Hairan" is a portmanteau: a word coined from a combination of the words "hair" and "Iran". It came to mind when I first read about Mahsa Amini.

[8] Iranian intellectuals and artists risk more than opprobrium by speaking out in public against the hard-line regime that rules the country; they risk losing their liberty and even their lives. For this reason, all poets when contacted by the editorial team were offered the opportunity to have their work published under a pseudonym or as "Anonymous". Although I was initially surprised that no one took up this offer, Ali Sobati assured me that *Hairan* represents an opportunity for female poets to have their voices heard on an international stage, and they would not dream of doing so anonymously, regardless of the risks. "Besides," Ali told me, "for the poets living inside Iran, it's probably more dangerous going to the street and demonstrating than it is having one poem translated and published in an anthology that will never be available inside Iran."

[9] This number is disputed, as Iranians are frequently counted based on their precise ethnicity. There are Iranian Arabs, Armenians, Assyrians, Azeris, Baluchs, Kurds, Lors, Persians, and Turkmens. Furthermore, migration for political reasons has been ongoing since the 1979 Islamic Revolution.

[10] On 25 June 2024, an article titled *"I begged them not to harass me": women accuse Taliban of sexual assault after arrest for "bad hijab"* (by Ahmad Ahmadi, Zahra Nader, and Farshid Aram) was published at *Zan Times* (https://zantimes.com). A few days later, on 3 July, *The Guardian* (https://www.theguardian.com) in partnership with *Rukhshana Media* (https://rukhshana.com) published a report titled *Video appears to show gang-rape of Afghan woman in a Taliban jail* (by Zahra Joya, Chris McGreal, Khudadad Poladi, Annie Kelly, and Tom Levitt).

زن.زیان.ئازادی | زن.زندگی.آزادی   WOMAN.LIFE.FREEDOM

Poster by Shaghaiegh Fakharzadeh.

INTRODUCTION BY ALI SOBATI

WITH ANAHITA REZAEI, SEPIDEH JODEYRI
& SEPIDEH KOUTI

THE SILENCED TRAJECTORY

The right to have a name and the right to name go hand
in hand. Perhaps this is why one stumbles into a Dune-
like, muted landscape when searching for the resonating
echoes of a feminine voice in the extra-millennial past of
Iranian poetry. There, at first glance, one is faced with a
lasting peculiar state: a double namelessness: a vast but
silenced realm of both names never heard and things
never named. This is the "silenced trajectory".

This simultaneous and systemic lack of recognition is
perhaps why, in the 1990s, Reza Barahani (1935–2022) –
a life-long radical [male] literary critic and theorist
– called for an "alternative womanly narrative". He
also offered a heavily interpretative and theoretical
manifesto to deconstruct *The Blind Owl*, by the [male]
writer Sadegh Hedayat (1903–51).[1] Originally published
in 1937, *The Blind Owl* is a short *mise en abyme* novel
that offers a surrealist/expressionist account (it owes
something to the early silent movies by Luis Buñuel
and F. W. Murnau) of characters decalcomaniacally
copy-and-pasted one into another. It is a widely held
belief among Iranian literary critics that *The Blind Owl*
is a founding modernist work in Farsi literature. And
thus, it is doubly problematic that in this novel female
characters are denied the right to bear a name or the
right to name – they are simply not allowed to speak for
themselves.

This situation, however, is by no means confined to
The Blind Owl, but rather is a paradigmatic one; it is
ascribable to almost the entire Iranian literary tradition
and history. For this reason, in Barahani's view, it was

time for women to use their voice and claim the right to narrate.

"Now it is time for the woman to become the narrator of her world and to do the naming herself," he wrote. "In literature, a woman's freedom means that she can define both herself and her surroundings."[2]

This, then, became the main historical quest and key aspiration among female Iranian writers: to break free from an imposed state of namelessness itself unnameable, the "silenced trajectory", that is deeply rooted in the fabric of our literary and poetic collective memory (or rather, our "collective amnesia").

"Our history," wrote Barahani, "in the course of centuries [...] has been a masculinised one – meaning it has been a history ruled over by the man: manly adventures, tyranny and oppression, justice and compassion, good and evil, lows and highs. The woman was never allowed to play any role, and that is why such history rarely has any feminine perspectives to offer."[3]

In opposition to this "silenced trajectory", Forough Farrokhzad (1934–67) – the Anne Sexton/Sylvia Plath of Iranian modern poetry – wrote:

Only the voice, the voice, the voice / The translucent demand of water to flow / The voice of sprinkling starlight on the feminine furrows of the earth / The voice of meaning being inseminated / And the jointly expanding love / The voice, the voice, the voice, it is only the voice that lasts...[4]

This introduction doesn't aspire to be a scholarly appraisal of Iranian women's poetry in all its dimensions. Rather, it is an attempt to give some historical context to the poems anthologised in this book. Most of these poems were composed (in Farsi) in response to unique social and political events in contemporary Iran: often, they are a tacit or direct response to the Woman Life Freedom (or WLF) movement, which grew out of Mahsa Amini's death in September 2022 – for not wearing her hijab in the officially prescribed way. The poems either elegiacally mourn Iran's fallen heroes – lost during an ultra-violent crackdown by the regime – or they celebrate the phenomenal bravery of women and girls, as well as the courage of many fearlessly supportive men.

And even if not connected to WLF events, the poems still speak to other contemporary sociopolitical events and tragedies in Iran, and almost always from a feminist standpoint.

Thus, in this introduction, through a number of carefully selected examples presented within three highly generalised periods (the classical, transitional, and modern-contemporary) we aim to give the overarching historical context of the poems in the anthology, without which it would be difficult for the general non-Iranian reader to relate to them.

THE AGE OF ORIGINS: THE POST-ISLAMIC, CLASSICAL PERIOD

The originary points of Iranian women's poetry are rather blurred. This is due to the imposed "silenced trajectory", that leaves us with little to no evidence and often with centuries-long holes in what evidence is available.

This lack is such that there are only two short surviving poems by the first historically recorded Iranian woman poet, and these are not in Farsi, the language she wrote in, but translated into Japanese and contained in an old poetry collection.[5] Daray Dokht was born in Japan in 661, since her father, Daray, was the king of a region that is north of today's Afghanistan; he had taken refuge there after the Arabs besieged Iran. There is a literary disagreement still in progress, however, whether Daray was actually the first Farsi-writing female poet, or whether this accolade should go to Zobeydeh bent al Ja'far (766–831, and also known as Zobeydeh Hashemiyeh).

Returning to Daray Dokht: she was the royal spouse of Haroun al Rashid, of the Abbasid Caliphate. Furthermore, the meaning and theme of her two translationally surviving poems is also disputed, especially regarding how profoundly they touch on Zoroastrianism – or alternatively whether they should be read as elegiac poems mourning the death of her husband.[6] Beyond their extra-textual references, they read:

> Even the fire set ablaze / Will seize and hide in its store / The thoughtful prophecy of the ancestors / Would they say such not?

> The Azure cloud / Hanging from the Northern Mountain / Passes through the stars / And through the moon / The Highest Heaven.

It is only from the tenth century onwards, however – the era of the prominent literary figure and Sufist poet, Rabia (also written as Rabe'eh) Balkhi (914–943) – that textual evidence survives – along with inaccurate and disputable accounts of her Sufistic and poetic status written by male literary historians and mystics – offering some limited but distorted insight into the long-denied contribution of women in Iranian poetry. Poetry aside, Rabia was also an accomplished illustrator, swordswoman and horsewoman, described in a literary biography composed a century after her death as: "the daughter of Ka'b, although a woman, was superior to men in accomplishments. She possessed great intelligence and a sharp temperament. She used to continuously play the game of love and admired beautiful youths."[7]

Even though there is no surviving collection of poetry by Rabia – and she is mostly [mis]represented and quoted by men in secondary literary sources – some of her verse has survived intact:

I bid my body was told of my soul / I bid my soul back to my body, with no cajole / I bid I could grow out of you intact / Alas! How to grow out of an inner hole?

Despite all the distortions and the imposed "silenced trajectory", this is the period in which verse with a starkly differing feminine tonality, approach and discourse is encountered for the first time. Such as this satirical poem by Manijeh Gha'ani Khowrasani (11th–12th century), meant as a retort to her tyrannical husband:

I will divorce you, setting myself free / Two husbands I take instead, a serendipitous jubilee / A one who is fresh and jejune / The other one being a Turkman goon / The former I hold near to mate / The latter I deliver to you out of hate.

Or even, more uniquely and expressly, this sexually explicit couplet by Mahsati Ganjavi (circa 1096–1181):

You bring your corroded cock and place it deep in my cunt / Kissing me on the perioral, so cunningly shameless and blunt;

Mahsati, who lived during the Qaznavid dynasty (977–1186), is considered by some critics as one of the two greatest couplet writers of Iran; the second is Khayyam. Some of Mahsati's compositions proffer such stark differences from the mainstream masculine

dictum of the time that it is impossible to ascribe to
them a manly poetic gaze and voice:

> I am not to be domesticated by an old breath / Being
> kept in gloomy chambers is worse than death /
> The hair that chains heart after heart / Cannot be
> enchained in a ragged doll's house like a marionette;

What is of note here is that this assertive, pleasure-
seeking demand – clearly stated by a woman –
represents the reversal of the eroticisation of hair in
the male-dominated poetic tradition of Iran. Here,
it is the owner of the hair herself who writes, and it
is as if a candle briefly flickers in the darkness of the
"silenced trajectory". The poet refers to her hair and its
captivating effect not as an exterior object admired only
by male viewers, but as an internal power (or even a self-
empowering quality) with which a woman can captivate
a man, and then proudly deconstruct the masculine
gaze by writing poetry about it.[8]

The other important female poets of this classical
period should not go unmentioned here: firstly, Jahan
Malek Khatoun (1324–1384), a poet-princess from Shiraz:

> For how long one can wander heartlessly,
> beloved-free / For how long shall I live for others,
> discounting what befits me / For how long withering
> away in search of loving company? / The life oozed
> out of me without a rejuvenating courting spree.

and Aisha Moqarriyeh (before 1329), the most renowned
female couplet writer after Mahsati Ganjavi:

> Last night, all the night, the dearest, of whose
> sorrow even my heart is in flight / Those ill-speakers
> bad-mouthing behind you – may their fate be full
> of plight – / Were warning me of your loose faith in

the affairs of love / And testified my own heart to it eventually proving right.[9]

In an atmosphere of domineering patriarchal poetics (majestically presided over by Hafiz, the greatest of all Iranian poets; as well as by Obeyd Zakani, the grand satirist of the classical age) it is often quite difficult to clearly distinguish their womanly voices – but not entirely impossible either, as the above examples show.

THE TRANSITIONAL AGE:
QAJAR AND CONSTITUTIONAL REVOLUTION

During the reign of the Qajar dynasty (1789–1925) – the last years of which overlap with the Irananian Constitutional Revolution (1905–11)[10] – both poetic form and poetic content were still closely aligned with mainstream masculine poetry. Moreover, poetic composition is a rare privilege limited to female members of the royalty and families of note. Common people were essentially deprived of literacy, and thus generally restrained to the limits of oral culture; they lacked a written literary culture until much later.

By the time of Nasser-al din Shah – the Qajarid king who reigned for fifty years between 1848–96, and whose eventual assassination was considered as an immutable cry for radical modernising change – literate women would still compose their poetry in Masnavi: a long-form rhyming couplet poetic style that places an emphasis on Sufism and was common in Iranian classical poetry.

What remains of the literary endeavours of these women amounts to a collection of sonnets, mystic and religious poems, or versified encomiums in praise of kings and other court members, with not much gender-distinguishing features in them.

This is a characteristic that shapes most of the pre-modern literary heritage composed by women, itself another stark reminder of the "silenced trajectory", which was not simply silencing women's voices but also forcing them into self-censorship, self-denial, and self-misrepresentation in a rather Lady-Macbethian, self un-sexing manner. This can be felt in the following lines by Aqa Beygum Baji (1780–1832, pen-name "Touti"), who was one of the harem wives of the Fat'ali Shah of Qajar:

> Blessed be anyone neighbouring thee / So is the air about you fresh and free.

There is also the following example by Reshheh Esfahani (1783–?):

> With the hair of a new beloved once again / I am enamoured, restless of its where and when.

Among the women poets pre-dating the Constitutional Revolution, there is one prominent writer, Táhirih Qurrat al-'Ayn (1814 or 1817–52). She was also a women's rights activist and Bábi theologian.[11] Like Rabia before her, Táhirih was such an iconoclastic figure that she eventually paid the price of her rebellion with her life. Looking back on Táhirih from these contemporary Woman Life Freedom times, we note that she was among the very first Iranian woman to remove her hijab; furthermore, she unveiled herself during a ceremonial gathering of some of the leaders of the Bábi Faith. After this scandalous act, she was seen by the monarchical and religious authorities as a profound threat to both patriarchal and theocratic values; and, in this way, she became the first woman to be executed under Sharia Islamic penal law, accused of "corruption on earth". This is a charge that is still levelled against Iranian dissidents and political prisoners, including those involved in the WLF protests.

A poem ascribed to Táhirih, in which she melancholically refers to herself in the third person, reads:

Your love woven by the weary heart onto the depths of soul / Thread after thread, string by string, roll on roll / In her heart, Táhirih, sought after you to no avail / Page after page, layer by layer, veil on veil.[12]

By the time the Constitutional Revolution began, sociopolitical developments in Iran did not leave women's poetry unaffected. Indeed, a whole array of new notions and phrases – alongside themes of liberty and equality, but also nationalistic ones – started entering women's writing.

Among the poets of this time, Mehrtaj Rakhshan (1881–1974) stands out. She was among the pioneers of the Women's Movement in Iran, the founder of all-girl schools, and another poet who removed her hijab. In 1928, she wrote an article in *Alam-eh Nisvan* (The World of Women) in which she recommended the foundation of a "House of Aspiration" dedicated to training and empowering female prostitutes. In her view, prostitution was a vice for society as a whole to tackle, and the responsibility for changing the fate of its victimised women should be borne by all equally. Also including herself in the third person, she writes:

Women are not yet aware of their civil rights / Rakhshan would conquer through their will the gate of the heights.

There is also Zandokht Shirazi (1909–52), a poet, social pioneer, and advocate of freedom and women's rights. Beneath a photo of herself in which she appears hijab-free, she writes:

Your photo, looking all glaring and happy, unlike me /
Yet of hijab and wrappings, all set free;

Zandokht also discerned and protested the complicity
of laws written by men, and male-dominated social
structures used against women:

Since the law was placed on women by men /
They committed injustices to the former that they
named justice / If making laws was dependent on
women themselves / The world would be free of all
this prejudice.

More feministic in the contemporary sense, Fatemeh
Soltan Farahani (1903–post-1926) was another poet
of this period. She believed that Iran could only be
liberated through women's knowledge, abilities, and
authority:

As become educated the girls of the motherland /
They will implant the tomorrow with their own
hand.

And then there is Fakhr Ozma Arqun (1898–1966)   the
mother of the prominent freedom-seeking icon and
neoclassical poet, Simin Behbahani (1927–2014), a poet we
will explore in the next part of this introduction. Fakhr
was not only a poet, but also an advocate of women's
educational rights; she was a political activist, an expert
in Iranian music and literature, and she left behind poems
that are expressly political, demanding radical change in
governance. In this respect, Fakhr is similar to another
poet of this period, Nimtaj Salmasi (1906–89). Nimtaj
made similar political demands in her poetry for political
reform.

A more important poet, perhaps, was Shams
Kasmayi (1883–1961). She had conducted extensive

studies about the nature of Iranian society, and was familiar with the ideas of the most progressive Iranian intellectuals. Thanks to speaking Russian, she was also knowledgeable about the Russian Revolution. Shams advocated for women's rights, writing in the progressive papers of the time, such as *Iran-eh Now* (The Modern Iran). She was also one of the first poets who actively joined the battlefield of "the new and the old" in Farsi literature, explicitly calling her time "the age of liberty and days of emancipation".

Lastly in this period there was Parvin Etesami (1868–1902). She was one of the best known Iranian neoclassical poets. She wrote in an argumentative, conversational style, composing many poems championing women's rights in Iran:

> It is as if, in Iran, women were never citizens, having no sway / On her shoulders, all plights heavily do weigh / Her justice-seeking call left unanswered / This injustice was not concealed, but done in the bright light of day.

Yet, like many other female poets in Iran during this period, much of Parvin's work is composed in a faux masculine voice; it lacks a genuinely feminine tone. This can be considered a result of the same self-censorship, or un-sexing, as mentioned earlier.

THE AGE OF FEMINIST WRITING: PRE- AND POST-1979 REVOLUTION

It is not far-fetched to consider this period to be that in which the "silenced trajectory" is finally broken – giving way to the birth of womanly poetry with an inherent femininity. This is mainly because Iran accelerated its modernisation process. This was dictated by the Pahlavid dynasty authorities, as well as through the exponentially increasing demands on the social bedrock. Consequently, women battled over and struggled for both means of and modes of expression. And their constant quest for self-expression led to a growing number of womanly poems. This period differs from previous ones because poetry composed by women sounds like it is; the murky patriarchal undertones of an essentially gender-alienating order don't affect this way of making poetry.

During this period – which is roughly coincident with the emergence of the second wave of feminism in the West, during the 1960s and 1970s – the dominant literature gradually paved the way for a fundamentally "other" feminine form of writing. This implies that the femininity of poetry transcended expressive content, topics, and themes, reaching into the profound structures of language and forms of expression. This resulted in the birth of a feminine voice that was previously unheard of.

As previously stated, it was through the poetry of Forough Farrokhzad that the "silenced trajectory" finally found a voice, and with such daring poems as *The Beloved*, where she openly describes a male lover:

> With his shameless naked body / Standing on his tough shanks / Like Death / With restless curvy lines / tracing his turbulent body / In its firm scheme / My lover / Looks like someone from generations long gone…;

And in a revealing conclusion:

> My lover / Has an unequivocal conception / Like nature itself / By defeating me / He endorses / The innocent rule of power.

From this point on, this novel approach to poetry becomes increasingly prominent – and to such an extent that the femininity of poetry composed by women becomes increasingly evident and inexorable. So much so, that Tahereh Saffarzadeh (1936–2008), a highly religious poet in many ways), commences one of her most renowned works: *A Love Journey.* Dedicated to Ali Shariati, one of the political ideologues of Shiite Islam, *A Love Journey* is composed in an unmistakably feminine and personal manner. Indeed, it begins with a reference to the poet Tahereh's hair:

> The sweeper noticed me ascending with my
> disarrayed wet hair from the river staircase,
> in the absence of daybreak.

Another example of the feminisation of poetic language can be observed by comparing two major neoclassical female poets mentioned earlier: Parvin Etesami and Simin Behbahani, the latter of whom rose to fame and recognition after the 1979 Iranian Revolution.[13] Parvin and Simin are both celebrated for their socially minded, justice-seeking poetry, and appreciated for their neoclassical poetic mastery. However, one rarely finds any textual evidence that Parvin's poetry was actually composed by a woman. On the other hand, there is plenty of textual evidence to be found in Simin's work demonstrating a self-aware, self-reflecting womanhood:

> To die not, you, the Gypsy, see silence to its perdition /
> Meaning to sing your own song, for being equates
> rendition / The dark ages long gone, heavily ossified
> around your body / You need to free from them, by a
> de-fossilising ambition;

It is important to note that the word "Gypsy" as used by Simin is a private symbol that frequently appears in her work; "Gypsy" represents a generic female figure, as well as the poet herself.

The "silenced trajectory" is addressed here as an impediment against womanly self-expression, but it also reveals an intricate correlation between bodily discrimination and the forced concealment of women's physicality. A piece of land long covered up and suffocated by the ossified strata of patriarchal traditional means and modes of expression – unable to be named or give name, to self-express – is presented metaphorically.

Similarly, this overhaul of feminisation was so overarching and far-reaching that it left almost no stone unturned, including that of the most abstract, obscure, and even mystic types of poetry composed by women. The poetry of Firouzeh Mizani (b. 1950), which was composed almost a decade before the 1979 Revolution, shows this process:

> Oh, you two, dark deer / Awake in the aurora pasture / Be gentler / For, till the drowsy dawn / – Of which remains but a single star – / Petunias are reciting my love poems / To the winds.[14]

At the core of this intrinsically charged imagery is the notion of sharing one's love experience with the natural world, a quality that is not unfamiliar to women's literary writing. For example, in the opening lines of a letter, amidst a profound and heated correspondence-based love affair between two of the greatest twentieth-century poets, Marina Tsvetaeva from Russia and the Austrian, Reiner Maria Rilke, Marina wrote: "I read your letter at the ocean; the ocean was reading along with me. We were both reading. I wonder if such a fellow reader troubles you. There won't be any others: I'm much too jealous (zealous – where you are concerned)."[15]

This poetic infusion with nature, through surging emotions, again brings to mind some of the most frequently quoted lines from Forough Farrokhzad's 1963 masterpiece, *Another Birth:*

I'm in love with your hands / I will plant mine in
the little garden / And I do know, I do know, they
will grow / And sparrows will lay eggs in the inky
furrows on my fingers / I will hang a pair of earrings
from my ears / Of Siamese blood-red cherries /
And will paste Dahlia petals onto my nails…

Such were the harbingers of unmistakable and
inescapable femininity, that the "silenced trajectory" was
finally cracking open. Historically speaking, before the
emergence of most paradigm-shifting, game-changing
sociopolitical transformations, one can trace them back
to a discursive level – to new ideas articulated in new
ways. In retrospect, we can see that the growth of the
feminine voice had already laid the groundwork for the
eventual rise of the Woman Life Freedom movement in
various forms of women's expression, poetry included.

   This pre- and post-revolutionary period roughly
coincides with the reign of the second and last Pahlavid
king, Muhammad Reza Shah (1919–80). Commonly
known as the Shah of Iran, he came to the throne in
1941. The post-revolutionary period began with his
dethronement in 1979, and spans the four decades that
have passed since then. It is in this atmosphere that
women – as poets as well as writers of prose – became
increasingly conscious of what was linguistically
alienating and misrepresenting. And it was in such a
spirit that in the 1990s and 2000s, poetic language was
feminised by women. All this took place at a time when
there was a relentless desire for experimental poetry in
general.

   What follows in this section, then, is an overview of
the multitude of women's voices that then appeared.

   In a clear continuation of her poetic confessional-
conversational style, Nazanin NezamShahidi (1954–2004,
a poet whose life, like that of Forough Farrokhzad, was
tragically cut short) in a poem published in 1993 writes:

Wipers / Wave hand / And it snows on the Tuesday. /
We wave hands: / – "Goodbye…" – / Wipers wipe /
The Tuesday snow / Off you / I wave hand / Wiping
your portrait / – "Goodbye…" – / It's snowing on the
empty road / And a pair of wipers / Throw themselves
in all insanity / From side to side / Of the throat /
Of mine, where it's snowing on your name;

"Tuesday snow" is experimental imagery, language
play – an increasing trend in women's poetry was to
become linguistically conscious when writing; the
pure materiality of language, too, became a legitimate
battleground for establishing newly risen voices.

In 1997, Granaz Mousavi (b. 1976) writes:

Even if I put on all clouds all over the world / They
still re-wrap me in covering gowns lest I'm exposed
nude / It is the dark side of the moon in here / The
slapping hand understands it not / That sometimes
the fish in the bowl / Can fall in love with a whale /
They scream at me to no avail / Understanding not /
I've already turned into a fish / With your river
having crossed through me / I'm not going to put on
all the deserts all around the world / And breathe
on a planet / Not yet observed / Even if they take the
wind to be fingerprinted / They won't trace your kiss
marks / One should go to the alley / Even though
cars open a gap between us and the sunlight / One
should go to the alley / This much sky isn't going to
be framed by the window / I need to sunbathe in the
southernmost corner of the soul.

Such writing not only exhibits a conversational and
confessional tone, but also an experimentalist character;
meanwhile the intimate topos suggest making the
case that now poetry composed by women constitutes
womanly writing. In this way, women's poetry from

this period onward becomes increasingly self-aware: not only of the right to have a name, but also the right to name. This is tellingly summed up in the title of Granaz Mousavi's volume of poetry published in 2002: *The Songs of an Unauthorised Woman.*

Another volume of poetry in the same vein from this period is *Annotations on the Domestic Wall*, by Pegah Ahmadi (b. 1974). It was received in the early 2000s as a poetry manifesto that radically questioned poetic givens:

> Here, by Shah Mosque / In a black chador / My hearty chamber cornering itself hermit-ly in the painful and rational / And am I happy in this store? / Brooming a woman's citizenry hair / Released into the night like a half-eaten peach.[16]

As alluded to by the title, this is a poem that endeavours (as if chasing an invisible target) to trace and deconstruct the same long-standing "silenced trajectory", by rereading an entire complex of canonically established historical texts and figures. The challenge here is to confront the language of poetry, while poeticising femininity; that is, writing poetry about a long-denied, long-neglected womanhood, but in a womanly manner. Elsewhere, the same poet writes:

> And I / With her entire dynasty turned dark, / Am history! / With black hair, since / Black is my earth, since / Black is my balcony / With amulets and table of indecipherable pins![17]

Here, womanhood is not taken as a historically silenced entity, but as a dark and silenced history in itself – it is the same history discussed here through a chain of chronicled examples, the same "silenced trajectory" revisited, the same double-edged lack to be once again challenged: the lack of the right to name, and the lack of right to name, while becoming aware of a history that has long suffered under the spell of patriarchal traditions and an omnipresent overlying time-(dis) honoured gender apartheid, a history passed in near-absolute darkness. This reminds us of the undiscovered and thus dangerous darkness perceived to be akin to the depths of Africa, as described in *Le Rire de la Méduse* (The Laugh of Medusa), by the French feminist critic and author, Hélène Cixous.[18]

No stone is left unturned, and this unprecedented feminisation of poetry stretches from imagery to syntax, from perspective to narrative.

Another well-known example is the lengthy poem, *I've Brewed Coffee To Carry On This Detective Story* (2001), by Rosa Jamali. Within it, one finds a genre-escaping, shape-shifting narrative, paired with cinematic techniques and terminology set amidst the atmosphere of a *film noir* detective story:

> Take one: / My hair a bit exposed out of the scarf / They said that woman had memorised the shape of the dishes by heart / Her buttons falling restlessly / And her heart a fallen * / Did you steal my dream when turning in reverse? / My first love poem, forgotten / Your code name, forgotten / The first word I ever uttered, forgotten / Even my ID, forgotten / Tell me the truth, did you steal my name?

The final lines suggest a radical questioning of the given that goes well beyond the mere content of poetry, its theme or topic, its aboutness. Here even one's given name is sceptically questioned as a misnomer, a name imposed, stealing one's own identity (the same challenge over lacking the right to have a name, and the right to give name). However, in poetry and elsewhere, this radical scepticism accelerates into such a forceful status that it can be traced across various generations and poetic styles.

For instance, Fereshteh Sari (b. 1956, a renowned poet and author, included on p. 124 of this anthology) writes in a poem published in 2008:

> I've dreamt that my name was squashed into stones bouncing back and forth / As if a white ball on a tennis table / And the situation wasn't such for me to ask / How is it that my name, being a proper noun / Has turned into a white ball;

The endeavour is to break the silence of the "silenced trajectory", to self-empower and win the right to have a name and to name. This is echoed in the following example by Saideh Keshavarzi (b. 1986, included on p. 195 of this anthology) in a volume of poetry revealingly titled *Communicating in Savage Sounds*:

> I'm a gesture / Obscenely zoomed in as communication wears off / I am imitating the throat, suffocated sounds / And was I turned into a voice, its syllables fall to the ground from my lips / Be communication with me. [19]

THE AGE OF WOMAN LIFE FREEDOM: THIS ANTHOLOGY'S CONTEMPORARIES

The history so far sketched out in this introduction is but a brief account of a centuries-long struggle that is still taking place: the struggle over the right to have a name, and to name; to break the never-ending spell of the "silenced trajectory". We hope that by presenting this history in such a way, however, the poems in the body of this anthology are more contextualised and thus more relatable to for a non-Iranian audience.

The concrete plurality of such distinguished literary voices profoundly resonates with the momentum of the Woman Life Freedom feminist uprising – not only in Iran but in the entire region. This highly consequential, but largely unanticipated, uprising occurred most forcefully between 2022–23. The crackdown against it, even by the standards of the brutal theocratic regime that rules Iran, has been extreme: over 22,000 arrested; more than five hundred reported deaths, including of seventy-one children; various types of child abuse; with all this accompanied by a glut of torture, execution and injury.[20]

Despite the commonly fabricated narrative in the mainstream international media (that stands almost entirely in opposition to the Iranian theocratic regime), WLF was not conceived in a context-free vacuum; it did not arrive out of thin air after the murder of Mahsa Amini. The struggle for women's rights encompasses decades of accumulated emancipatory resistance. As a political term, the triangle of woman, life and freedom was originally theorised in the 1990s by Abdullah Öcalan, one of the founding members of the Kurdistan Workers' Party (PKK). He is a Kurdish dissident political leader and intellectual born in Turkey, and a life-long political prisoner of the Turkish state. He believed that women were under the oppression of a patriarchal order, in addition to that of capitalism and the nation-state. He considered women to be "the first subjugated nation in history"; that "woman is an occupied land that has to be unoccupied". He went so far as to ask men in his society to end the oppression of women, figuratively demanding that they "kill the masculinity in themselves". "Society will never be emancipated as long as women are not." "Woman, life, freedom means a free woman, a free land, and even a free man," he stated.[21]

Even though the slogan "Woman Life Freedom" eventually became the movement's key motif, chanted by women all over Iran, its ideas have been looming over the Middle East long before 2022. The slogan has been shouted by justice-seeking "Saturday Mothers" in Turkey; by the Kurdish guerilla women of Kobani in the autonomously ruled Kurdish regions of Syria, called Rojava; during the relentless battles to the break the grip of ISIS; and by the women of Afghanistan after their country was reconquered by the Taliban.

Woman Life Freedom's ability to surpass all national boundaries lies in its high degree of translatability into a basic condition of de-subjugation. To provide an illustration: during the course of the WLF movement in Iran, one of the prominent leftist political theoreticians and academics of philosophy in exile, Mohammad'Reza Nikfar, published a series of essays on Radio Zamaneh, a Farsi-leaning opposition website based abroad and affiliated with the government of the Netherlands. Nikfar emphasised the "intersectional" and thus quickly expandable nature of this slogan, and the fact that WLF rose vehemently against the idea of minorities in particular, who are regarded as un-autonomous and therefore inferior subjects. Thus, its emancipatory call was able to include gender minorities, women and queers, ethnic minorities such as Kurds, and religious minorities such as Sunni Muslims in Baluchistan, who participated in protesting mass prayers in their main religious city, Zahedan.[22]

What is becoming increasingly clear, is that the struggle at the centre of the whole literary history of Iranian women's poetry coincides with the equally fierce and long-standing struggle that resulted in WLF: womanly voices trying to break away from the "silenced trajectory". The poetry in this anthology reveals the struggle against the patriarchal, homogeneity-seeking regime in terms of the language that governs the "normalisation" of poetic grammar, as well as that of a dominant socio-political order reigned over by a self-proclaimed, supreme leadership with boundless authority and assumed superiority over any form of "otherness". This is why the bulk of references or allusions made by many of the poems collected here to certain events or figures of WLF have been explained in footnotes. Taken together, these poems and their notes shed light on the dark corners of this immensely proud, unstoppable historical moment where – for the first time, on such a vast scale, and in a country ruled by pious old men – women set their mandatory hijab on fire in the most visible public arenas of even the most religious and conservative cities.

The interconnectedness of poetry and the revolutionary movement is such that one can discern it on multiple levels. The most immediately relevant level is found in such poems as *This Place* (p.73); it was composed in Evin Prison after the poet was arrested, tried, and sentenced for her solidarity with the WLF movement. This is a fate shared by other poets in this book, including Aida Amidi, author of *The Fish* (p.79). Aida was on the board of the Iranian Writers' Association when she was arrested along with a group of other members. In addition, there are numerous poems explicitly celebrating the rise of the WLF movement: such as *For Mahsa Amini* (p.221) and *Are You Asleep?* (p.222). Other poems honour the innocent lives taken in the course of the movement: *Jina* (p.92). as well as Nazanin Ayghani's elegy to the same person (p.172). Or in another elegy to Mahsa Amini, *Do Create* (p.112\ composed by Farkhondeh Hajizadeh – with its poet having one of the most shocking backstories recounted in a footnote below her poem. Farkhondeh dedicated her poem to Khodanour Lojjeyi, a young Baluchi protester who was shot dead in Zahedan's Bloody Friday massacre; that event is also explained in footnotes.

There are socially concerned and politically minded poems related to historical tragedies that occurred before the rise of the WLF movement. Such as *Captivated Breaths* (p. 180), dedicated to Baktash Abtin – a poet, activist, documentary filmmaker and key member of the Iranian Writers' Association – who passed away a year before the rise of this movement after the authorities ignored his COVID-19 infection while in prison.

And then there is the link between many of the poems anthologised here and the issue of the mandatory hijab, and hair itself:

– 'cause my hair aches (p. 62)
All an error no wider than a thin strand of hair (p. 64)
The land of hair-gallowing Eves (p. 85)
And the snow, sitting on her hair / Is my hell! (p. 87)

Or less explicitly in *Do You Recall Playing With My Hair?* (p. 102).

All the imagery, themes, references, and tropes pertaining to hair found in this anthology relegate women's hair to various levels of experience: hair as a sentient organ, hair as a symbol of mourning, rage, and hope. The issue of hair extends far beyond the relatively straightforward inquiry into whether women should be compelled to wear the hijab or not. It represents the struggle women have had against being violently disadvantaged and systemically discriminated against, being disenfranchised, devalued, and considered inferior, less mature, and not capable of having their own bodily autonomy. From a poetic standpoint, the interrelated matter of hijab and hair brings us back to the issue of being denied both a name and naming.

But the question of mandatory hijab does not sum up the entire literary struggle, since the rest of women's bodies also constitute a battle-zone much larger than the head alone. The body is poetically present in this anthology as a phenomenological site of lived experiences; it is an inner lingual pantheon on whose walls one finds the bass reliefs of horror, denial, rejection, suppression, murder, and obliteration; it is a site in which all condensed historical nightmares are re-encoded and where corporeality and subjectivity overlap. This often proceeds from a simple daily experience, as in:

> I am satiated / With a tea (p.94)

And from there the poem grows into eerie encounters where catastrophe lurks:

> My mouth is sweetened / And sweet is the blood / Spilled in protest marches

Furthermore, at times, poetry is daring enough to study power erotically, libidinously, and in its pure physicality – where a feminine Eros is literally faced with a masculine Thanatos:

> I say my name through the vaginal void of the word / When the radius of my tongue / Was thickened in a phallic circle of demise (p.96)

On p.111, one can read:

> You grew old / And your mouth, opened in the form of a kiss / Came together, tight, / On the lips of death

There is a triangular relationship between eroticism, power and language that is sometimes forthright and shocking:

> I have lexically wetted myself from head to toe (p.104)

While at other times, it points to the tie between seasonal freshness, rejuvenation, and womanhood:

You said / Don't write poems / Be a woman /
Then life itself becomes poetic (p. 100)

Moreover, in some poems there is a sort of coming to a
womanly consciousness – a moment of self-realisation
– through the very particularity of a day-to-day
experience. We experience this in *The Standing Figurine*
(p. 108):

You were standing / With your basic urge for
makeup / Covered in mascara / Dripping down
from your eyes / In a politically teary gesture

Here is a mode of, say, epiphany revisited, with the
speaker only realising upon narrating her unwontedly
imposed political situation as a citizen made second-
class through her corporeal, every-day, urban and
mundane presence.

At other times, womanly consciousness takes a more
imperative and assertive stance:

Harken the magic revolt in my insurgency / That
made the waters unquiet / Harken the wanton
thunderbolt in my eye (p. 48)

Or in another poem:

Fear me, as I become a woman / As I become of
no man! (p. 119)

In certain cases, like in the satirical poem *Dear God*
(p. 160), the occupying omnipresence of the divine
in a middle-class woman's domestic life is ironically
questioned. Different in style but similar in message,
there is a neoclassical sonnet by Fatemeh Ekhtesari
(p. 117) – herself a political and literary refugee based in
Europe for many years – where, bitterly, one reads:

On Friday, instead of birth control / Got kicked and punched around, heart-whole / On Saturday, instead of birth control / I said "No", and again the beating loophole.

This anthology is highly diverse, with a somewhat Bakhtinian, carnivalesque tone: a multitude of voices irreducibly pluralistic, heterogeneous, and singular. Thus, there are poems with a much higher degree of aesthetic abstraction, but with their own unique womanly voice, such as *A Rotating Absence* (p. 81), by Ailin Fattahi:

Which finds no sign of form in memory / It is your fingerprint / Bifurcated in your absence / Erased but still recalling / Recalling but erasable / Erased and recalled, but / Not turned to absence in an absence of its own / It retains an eerie absence to itself / And returns / A purely formless form

Or Banafsheh Farisabadi's poem, *It's Always About A Bird* (p. 88):

If we take it to be a bird / If we open its heavy wings wide with two indecisive thumbs / Heavy circles engaged, you could say night blind, / Where should they be suspended to flesh out death?

Then there are those poems that articulate this womanly consciousness in their linguistic performance alone, such as in Leila Sadeghi's poem, *Freedominance* (p. 138):

Horses hoofing in a millennial siege / Forever freedominating, for ever-freedominance / Tell of the long showering hair as I rise against your death / Tell of the historiest passage to all the blood shed in its name / Of the girl fiddlesticking bone on hair.

IN CONCLUSION

The purpose of this introduction has been to demonstrate how Iranian women poets have suffered from a centuries-long subjugation – in the sense of not being able to fully express themselves. Women were mostly denied the right to have a name or give one. This denial was either outright, through prohibition – or by being socially pressured into imitating a masculine voice; women could write, but in disguise.

Iran's feminine literary history thus contains a dense misogynistic streak: which we have called the "silenced trajectory", which only started to crack open under the rush of modernisation in the twentieth century. It was at this point that women started to express themselves in a womanly voice.

This anthology beautifully captures the latest stage of women's poetic autonomy in Iran. And it is no exaggeration to say that this has occurred (and is occurring) in response to and motivated by the most groundbreaking, bravest feminist movement in the history of modern Iran and perhaps the world: Woman Life Freedom.

[1] *The Blind Owl* by Sadegh Hedayat is available in an English-language translation by D. P. Costello (2010, Grove Atlantic, New York).

[2] Reza Barahani, *A Report to the Age Free Coming Generation,* 1995, Markaz Publishing, Tehran.

[3] Ibid., *The Masculinised History: The Ruling Culture and Culture under Rule, Part II,* 1984, Avval Publishing, Tehran.

[4] All poem excerpts and verses quoted in this introduction were translated by Ali Sobati.

[5] These poems can be found in *Man'yōshū,* the oldest collection of poetry ever assembled in Japan. It contains over 4,500 poems by poets from various royal and social classes. Compilation ended in the second half of the eighth century.

[6] Zoroastrianism originated in ancient Persia six centuries BCE, thus also predating Islam by about 1,200 years. Principally, this monotheistic religion (Zoroaster is regarded as a prophet of the one God) teaches that humans must choose between good and evil, and that they have the free will to follow either Ahura Mazda on the side of good, or Angra Mainyu (also known as Ahriman) who represents evil. There are still more than 100,000 Zoroastrians practising the religion worldwide, although their numbers are declining, since converting to the faith is no longer encouraged.

[7] *Sufi Women of South Asia: Veiled Friends of God,* Tahera Aftab, 2022, Brill Academic Publishers, Leiden. Also see *The Story of Rabia Balkhi, Afghanistan's Most Famous Female Poet:* https://ajammc.com/2021/08/16/rabia-balkhi-afghanistan-poet, 16 August 2021.

[8] A similar but much older key literary moment can be found in Ferdowsi's *The Book of Kings* (Shahnameh), in the tragic filicidal tale of the clash between Rostam, the legendary hero of Iran, and his juvenile but equally strong son, Sohrab. The latter was fighting against his father when leading the Turkish enemy army in their assault on Iran. Neither of the two opponents knew the identity of the other. This tale has been described at length where relevant in the body of this anthology. A heroic woman called Gordafarid is a formidable opponent for Sohrab before battle. She is eventually defeated by Sohrab, however, and is forced to engineer her release by removing her helmet and revealing her long hair and beautiful face. The Book of Kings contains many similar examples of power-switching between men and women, and for this reason, it has become a rich source for feminist re-interpretation of ancient Iran; hence, the multiple references in this anthology to key female figures in this ancient epic work: such as Tahmineh, in Bita Malakouti's poem, *Jîna* (p. 92), and Roudabeh, in Samiranik Norouzi's poem, *From Herat School To Tehran* (p. 198). As regards this whole subject, the best scholarly text available in English is *Women in the Shahnameh, Their History and Social Status Within the Framework of Ancient and Medieval Sources,* Djalal Khaleghi Motlagh, edited by Dr. Nahid Pirnazar, translated by Brigitte Neuenschwander, published online by Cambridge University Press, 1 January 2022.

[9] Seyyed Ali Mirafzali is an expert on contemporary Iranian couplets. He claims on his weblog (http://mirafzali.blogfa.com) that he has come across two poignant satirical couplets by Aisha that mark unprecedented outspokenness similar to that displayed by Mahsati Ganjavi.

[10] The Constitutional Revolution of Iran led to the establishment of a parliament after the Constitution was signed in 1906. This was a transformative moment in the history of Persia/Iran, and it has been

cited as the first event of its kind in the Islamic world. Women, and various groups formed by women, played a dynamic role in efforts to reform Persian society. Sadly, however, many vital issues directly affecting Persian women were left out of the Constitution, and women were denied the right to vote (alongside certain convicted criminals).

[11] Bábism, or the Bábi Faith, was founded in Iran in 1844 by the Báb (b. 'Ali Muhammad); he was an Iranian merchant who professed himself to be a prophet of God. The foundations of the religion are monotheistic, but Bábism was seen as a threat to Shiite Islam and violently crushed. After his public execution in 1850, the Báb's mortal remains were smuggled out of Iran and interred in Haifa, in what was then Ottoman-ruled Palestine.

[12] In the Iranian classical verse form known as *ghazal* (close to the idea of the Western sonnet), poets often introduce their name in the third person into the verse; this is a device called *tajrid* (abstraction). Hence, the appearance of "Táhirih" in the last line of this example, as well as "Rakhshan" in a verse on p. 31.

[13] Simin Behbahani was an ardent feminist who risked her life to champion women's rights in Iran. She was the representative of the most systematic feminist campaign launched after the 1979 Revolution in Iran – known as the One Million Signature campaign. For these efforts, she received the feminist Simone de Beauvoir Prize in 2009. The campaign resulted in imprisonment, security threats and surveillance of campaign participants by the regime's security forces.

[14] Even though the title of this poem by Firouzeh Mizani is commonly translated as *The Rebirth*, this rendition loses an important meaning, since the poem does not communicate being born again as a second chance of appreciating the world, but rather as a radical metamorphosis into a genuine existential femininity/womanliness. Firouzeh Mizani is considered part of what has been called the Pure Poetry movement, which originated in southern Iran.

[15] Quoted in *Reading Letters Summer 1926: Boris Pasternak, Marina Tsvetayeva, Rainer Maria Rilke,* Carla Baricz, Ploughshares at Emerson College: https://blog.pshares.org/reading-letters-summer-1926-boris-pasternak-marina-tsvetayeva-rainer-maria-rilke.

[16] The Shah Mosque is located in Isfahan, in central Iran. It is on the south side of Naghsh-e Jahan Square. Construction started in 1611, under the orders of Shah Abbas I. The mosque is regarded as a masterpiece of Persian architecture.

[17] From the poem, *You, the Granter,* found on the online literary magazine, *Davat:* http://www.rezaghassemi.com.

[18] Hélène Cixous is a French writer, playwright, and critic of literature. In 1969, she established the first centre for women's studies at Centre

universitaire de Vincennes, Paris. Her feminist text dealing with women's writing, *The Laugh of Medusa,* was published in English in 1976 by the University of Chicago. It can currently be read at https://www.jstor.org/stable/3173239. Drawing a geographic-cultural parallel with Africa, Cixous explains that in much the same way as what was called "the dark continent", the female mind and body has historically been viewed as undiscovered, unexplored, and therefore dangerous – "dark" in that sense. Translated from the French by Keith and Paula Cohen, *The Laugh of Medusa* begins: I shall speak about women's writing: *about what it will do.* Woman must write her self [sic]: must write about women and bring women to writing, from which they have been driven away as violently as from their bodies […].

[19] This poem was originally published on the poet's weblog (http://gahi.blogfa.com). It was subsequently published in a poetry volume bearing the same title as the poem: Saideh Keshavarzi, *Communicating in Savage Sounds,* 2017, Afraz Publishing, Tehran.

[20] For a more thorough understanding of the various dimensions of the Woman Life Freedom movement, see a report published on 12 October 2022 on the Iranian Human Right Activists News Agency website: https://www.en-hrana.org/woman-life-freedom-comprehensive-report-of-20-days-of-protest-across-iran.

[21] *Woman Life Freedom: from A Lonely Man in Isolated Confinement to the Streets of Iran,* Souzan Ghorbani, published on 14 October 2022 on https://www.bbc.com/persian/articles/cqq6yev5kxwo.

[22] *WLF: The Beginning of a Revolution? What is Going on in Iran?, Part II,* Mohammad'Reza Nikfar, Radio Zamaneh, on https://www.radiozamaneh.com/735810.

INDEX TO THE POETRY (alphabetically by author)

POEMS

Translator's note: The punctuation of verse translated for this anthology follows that used by the poets writing in Farsi. Many stanzas, and indeed poems, end with no punctuation.

IN GREY AIR
Afrouz Kazemzadeh

In grey air
With trousers inside out
I stood there in front of Germany's embassy

– 'cause my hair aches
Since I was twelve
In the old man's hand

My mouth open to emancipation
My hair aching by the Middle East
By you
By a world that
Swings back and forth among kitsch dolls.

When death stood on the launch pad
My hair held hostage
No ice melted on my body ever again
Must turn away
Riding a horse
Lest the sea
Freezes to death behind me.

Did you know?
I gallop ahead
And the sea, frozen behind me.
Haven't you ever seen?
Haven't you ever heard
Of a sea frozen,
Behind aching hair?

You don't know
When my hair aches
And my body held hostage
The sea not forgetting frozenness
And I!
Turned into a tigress uneducated to rip apart
Amidst the aching hair
And I!
Could only think of a cloud
The one with no hair.

And how would you know
The ache in your hair
Being extended in grey?

I wake up every morning on a bed of hair
Locked into aching
And throw up the night
In a broken loo.

Nothing is green
I will never turn green.

Even the heat of the drier
The darkening on my body
And mismatched rugs
Would turn my naiveties green.

I'm just a tigress
Sleeping in the Middle East's hair!

STREET TRILOGY
Afsaneh Nojoumi

Author's dedication: To the brave women of my country.

I

Now, all an error no wider than a thin strand of hair[1]
Even the narrative that clenches
A floating humid in a humidity afloat,
Onto geometrical capillaries of a woman
In the suicidal age of Life held under the street's nose
That one day pitched to dance in a calligraphy
   composed, mummified, in wordy intervals
So that seasons binge
As they hinge on the mirror's joints, splashed on an
   ogling vase exposed to a mythical whirlpool
As the temple splashes out and then bodied in light
By my womanly tongue,
I destratify the alley's contemporary bruise from
   cadaverous infections!

II

From thunder to street
From street to thunder and contrariwise
Runnable indeed, a river to be crossed on every eve
Inhuming the alley's drought
To find in floating saliva, debris of marshy hands
Whose infected shadow a barrage pressing against
   the lips
Recall the throat vaporised in mourning.
Now, back to mirror
So that illuminated darks radiate crow and bone
Papers crumpled
Blowing into denser sentences, with organs glued into
   tussaphobia in a window's clutched jaws

The pores of these lines, set afloat
 In the dark radiance of lips dripping from the eve
And if you multiply the voice
You can spot
The alley suspended, bleeding up to its knees, running
   in waves' torsos
I dragged hailstones out of photos
The street wrapped its secondary pauses in newspaper
   senses
May it be blistered by natural sound fabrics in a
   pronounced horizon on the eve over dictated gems
Standing on a netted gap as objects turn aggressive
Meandered, against a night that carries on.

III

I remember you in side-view, during a delirious
   afternoon
In a photo's straps wearing a vested instinct
Whose feminine fragrance
Accelerated past
The line of box trees attached to nocturnal influx
Recall that sophisticated pause wrapped in circulating
   letters.
And enclosed, flanked in your hair
In thunder that pulsates blood through bone pores
I arise from the mirror, and your voice
Which, in the burnishing chips of this eve,
From universal hands blowing dusty downpours into
   the soil
To wanderings covered in woe, from head to toe
Sowing thunderclaps of fingers spattered all over the
   street's throat
And an ode to shed the light of your radiant facial sketch
On coughing walls dragged to intense trachoma
In the weeping accent of your hair
Now that the street's sonata is no wider than a thin
   strand of your hair!

NOTE: STREET TRILOGY (previous pages)

[1] In Farsi, when it is said that something "depends on a strand of hair" it means that it is very risky, or finely balanced. In English, one might say "skating on thin ice". However, when Mahsa Amini – the young Iranian woman whose death inspired the Woman Life Freedom movement – was murdered by the so-called morality police because her hair was not covered in accordance with Iran's hijab laws, this Farsi expression was updated. People now say: "Mahsa, after you, everything hangs by a strand of hair." Graffiti of this expression was photographed, and the slogan went viral.

WE'LL COME BACK TO PICK WILD ROSES[1]
Anahita Rezaei

Tonight, the exegesis of pardon,
Is upon the throat's intercession
Since in Khavaran,[2]
Tonight,
After solar vertigo
Is past round eighteen
Pardon!
For how probable the eclipse
For the massacre of roaches
In managed escalation
For sulphur, poignant in the air
Accusing the mountain-climb
Created martyrs
In monsoon storms
Of the Alborz mountain range[3]
Every year, for no reason
Pardon!
I'm a woman, pardon!
With no reserved chest
In Victoria's Secret demi bras
Without chorea
Matching the sex organs
That – a macho pedestrian of Thursday eves – would…
   you amply
Without dreams dreamy enough for the eyes,
In the rigid dark of an ominous night
Un-tanned, from beneath my
Tattoo, worn out
By the bullet crossing:
Kouey Daneshgah![4]

CONT'D OVERLEAF

Tonight, when Khavaran is
Decorated by light!
Lit by tallow-burner candles,
With scanning eyes!

I'm a doctor, pardon!
With pocket-bound hands,
With cemented gloves
Rendered helpless
Patrolled by death, at most leisure times
Despite the simplicity
Pardon! My bad!
That Tehran is leaden
By imported real McCoy
So this very thing's sediment in brain and guts
Infiltrates my father's death into memory
Pardon that I'm sedimenting along the night
Without Said Kangarani[5]

Here, where Tehran
Is under assault
By rallying cabs

An insomniac twenty-four hours in February 1979[6]
What remains of it today,
Only a cigarette brand[7]
I infiltrate into channels locked
Without passport, pardon!
Pardon for the mute calligraphy
For error alarms in banking ATM systems
For street-sweepers' dogma in collecting garbage
For Sohrab.[8]
In a death, *mano a mano*[9]
For the praiseworthiest...

Tonight, in Khavaran, nomadic songs
Are ceaselessly sung.

[1] An allusion to a novel with the same title written by the French author, Jean Lafitte.

[2] Khavaran, in Tehran, is a cemetery where the remains of countless political prisoners are interred in unmarked graves. These political detainees were executed by the Islamic regime during the 1980s. To this day, Khavaran is a conflict zone where frequent clashes occur between families in mourning but seeking justice, and state security forces and mercenaries paid by the regime.

[3] A group of mountains in northern Iran that runs from the border of Azerbaijan to the western and southern parts of the Caspian Sea. It ends in the northeast of the country, where it joins up with the Aladagh Mountains. In the northern part of Khorasan, it borders a mountain called Kopet Dag.

[4] One of the principal student residential areas of Tehran University. This has always been the main site of student resistance and protests against the regime. Brutal crackdowns on multiple generations of students occurred here in the 1990s, then in 2009 during the Green Movement protests, and finally during the Woman Life Freedom demonstrations that began in 2022 after the death of Mahsa Amini.

[5] A traditional Iranian singer of the post-1979 period, whose pro-revolutionary anthems from the early 1980s have always been popular, but also a source of political side-taking and much dispute.

[6] A reference to 11 February 1979, recognised as the day the Iranian Revolution (also called the Islamic Iranian Revolution) triumphed, resulting in the establishment of the current regime.

[7] In Iran, there is a brand of cigarettes called Bahman, meaning February. The name was chosen to commemorate the 1979 Revolution, which took place that month. The poem underlines the irony of this homonymity: none of the values and ideals that motivated the 1979 Revolution have endured, and the revolution's legacy has no more worth or value than a packet of cigarettes.

[8] This could refer to Sohrab, the mythical son of Rostam, who in a mishap of mutual recognition is killed by his father in one of the most significant tragedies in the classical epic, *Shahnameh* (The Book of Kings). It could also be a reference to Sohrab A'rabi – or any number of young male protesters who were killed by the regime during successive crackdowns. Sohrab was shot by plain-clothes security forces during the Green Movement protests in 2009. Sohrab became one of the key symbols of innocent bloodshed perpetrated by the regime during those protests – while his mother, Parvin, still seeks justice for her son and has become a thorn in the flesh of the regime.

[9] This means "hand-in-hand" in Spanish.

WHOSE LIFE WAS A BIRD!
Arezou Rezayi Mojaz

The *Kouseh'Barneshin* of magic moment[1]
With the sweet blessing weighing upon the
    neighbourhood
That turned you, a curio
Into the victim of nights!
You stretched up your neck
On your motherland's piggyback
With bird-aerial movements in the outspoken town
You look into the dark!

– What spring, given birth to by you!

Here, where blood,
Stains the scaffold
And mountain crimsons
Clotting on newly risen tulips
Our youth embossed!

– What spring, given birth to by you!

In a roasted corner
Where we remove
The suffering fingertips
Off fresh graves.
This be the Genesis
Whose roots
Grow from your crown
Weaving the umbilical cord
Strap after strap.

– What spring, given birth to by you!

The head, carried jointly
By all the crowd
Placed on a sparse neck,
Filled with voices:

"The flood is yours, sir!"

Where else
They do harken
History's youth
By anonymous dunes
With girlish lips?

– What spring, given birth to by you!

This rebelling body
In a hand-to-hand cell division
That showered voices in Enghelab Street wanders[2]
Showering voices on the cemented wings of
    Tehran University,
Showering voices on graveyard's freshness.

What spring, given birth to by you!
Here, where screams fear no more;
Letters by a womb, unfolding.

Ask those children who give birth to their mothers,
You, the inscriber of blank cartridges
Noted down on the street's corporality!

Ask trees' forelegs, standing yonder
And the bruised moment:
How you passed from summer to fall
When spring
With inadequate hands

CONT'D OVERLEAF

Was banging on an earthly gate
Asking with a womanly throat:
You, the light in my eye,
Will you allow me in?

---

[1] *Kouseh'Barneshin* was a ritualistic celebration of spring in pre-Islamic
Iran, during the Sassanid Empire. It involved a clean-shaven man
sitting on an ass and wandering the city with a fan in one hand and a
crow perched on the other. He sang songs to bid farewell to winter
and welcome spring, while collecting coins from onlookers. This
tradition still takes place today. It can be compared to the *Lupercalia*
celebration in ancient Rome, which was annually celebrated on
15 February, to cleanse the city and encourage good health and
fertility.

[2] One of the most important and historic streets in downtown Tehran.
The name, Enghelab, means "revolution", and was given to honour
the 1979 Iranian Islamic Revolution.

THIS PLACE
Atefeh Chaharmahalian[1]

Author's note: Composed in Evin Prison, on 9 December 2022.

This place
Now turned into the untimely throbbing of pain
And mourning flags
Have raised their cry to get past the bayonets' grip
The desolate bar of soap, grows thinner every day
Sniffing after the dark in judges
Turned haggard by waterfall, and dead ends of
   Valiasr Street
The city
Calls its murdered corners by name
A sea of those drowned, wells up into beliefs
So that a mother hymn
Re-embraces history.
We had no footing
For the path to let us stand
So that blood reaches the kiss of Truth
So that bars
Pass through the enflamed sparrows
Yet, our corpses, all animate
And our lips, to be hushed no more
After being placed before the squad of fire
We died in immense fertility
Even though our farming selves
Were the festive lands of wheat
And the wet-year blight
Swaddled our children in ailment
Even though the trial is capital in punishment
And its eyes
Blinking in iron
Its industrial ideals

CONT'D OVERLEAF

Worshipped at capitalising altars
Even though at hand
Is the night
Lo! You, the gloomy thirst
Place flowers on abandoned veins
Hang lanterns on ivies never grown
And do not relinquish the search
For that limitless light
So that in the street, stars
Morph into comets.

[1] Atefeh Chaharmahalian has published many volumes of poetry and is one of the most respected poets in Iran. She writes in a pure, abstract style, which is reflected in this poem. She is also a renowned activist and social worker. Like many other women poets, she was persecuted by the regime during the Woman Life Freedom protests. In October 2022, she was incarcerated in Evin Prison for seventy-one days, which included a prolonged period of solitary confinement. The fabricated case against her was finally quashed in February 2024. Evin Prison, in a suburb of Tehran, was originally built in 1972. It is one of the most feared prisons in the country. It has been nicknamed "Evin University" due to the large number of highly educated critics of the regime incarcerated there at any one time.

SOFT SPOTS
Atena Soleimani

Such soft sports you've got, the head!
How wet you are!
Such eyes and blood you've got
I started pondering from the day I was denied
    touching you
I uttered sounds unbeknownst to me
With no exterior to find
One night I watched over my blood in an estranged
    wilderness
One night, I was of the mood
And my hand couldn't clear the soil away
I was holding, with both hands, two contradictory cubs
Half-blood cubs bringing genitive justice into action.

Sights are but eyes
Faces safeguarded from their own drag
Separate is the head
Soft and separated, not knowing
That it's been dragging along
As it does today
Intention-free
Inside is distant
As is outside
My head is the snow on peaks
As is my landscape, the snow on peaks.

THE FISH
Aida Amidi

Author's note: Composed in 2016.

One day the light crosses through dark curtains again
And the slippery fish
Will settle down on your right shoulder
You smile
And my fingers' spirits
Will touch the corn

One day, I jump out of nightmares
And explore your hands
On my scarred forehead
I kiss the words and let them go unheard
And shut my eyes against the dark siege

Yet now
The slippery fish is crouching in shadows on the wall
Failing to remember
The day it'd lived
Under your moist skin

I had returned from many a wars
And old wounds wouldn't let me be
Threw my skin into fire
And created myself another skin
One slimy
Unable to breathe away from free waters
A skin that now
Carries the mark of your graceful teeth
Into the sea

CONT'D OVERLEAF

One day I'll return home
And in another pale eve
My fingers' spirits
Will drag your drifting head
Out of the rubble
And, at last,
You'll invest faith
In the voice of blood
Which runs in veins
Looking for life.

A ROTATING ABSENCE (abridged)
Ailin Fattahi

Street to street, next to pedestrians' footprints,
　　yours are of snow
An unreadable writing to be exposed patiently
　　against fire
There is your presence, yet, all in white
Gesture-less, unindicative
The unreadable solitarily open to reading
And two co-travellers' small talk on a winter's eve,
　　a photomontage
Foregrounded on a landscape as pale as it goes
Remaining there, as long as the thermometer leaps
So I want, as long as there is time,
To have registered this
And this
And this
On the faces of tiles
(And not the illustrations, but in cracks)

Which finds no sign of form in memory
It is your fingerprint
Bifurcated in your absence
Erased but still recalling
Recalling but erasable
Erased and recalled, but
Not turned to absence in an absence of its own
It retains an eerie absence to itself
And returns
A purely formless form
Under white carbon paper
This Persian absence.

CONT'D OVERLEAF　　　　　　　　　　　　　　　　　　81

And your trail
The fullest of temporal awareness
A chance for each absence to return
A move with ears fully equipped
And remaining staring into circulating lines
Unearthing the hidden angles of this absence
Which actually,
Happens
– in trompe l'oeil

Yet, there is your presence
White over white
As if chalk!
Big white pictures on the wall
The soul unreadable open to reading.

MOTHER EARTH
Azita Ghahreman

Lover's arms
Are rain.
With fingers of
Moist and spell
Opening the chest-lock of the earth
And then,
Mother's bodily aroma
Fills in the air bubbles.
Rejuvenated now,
The mother
With a fresh netted shawl and breezing veil
Tinkling on her,
A crimson-leafed anklet.
Passing through the garden
Dancingly, devotedly,
Whirling afar.
As stops the rain,
I see her again
On the last picturesque hill
Lying down
Bare and unbound
Wearing a rainbow
Around her neck.

GALLOWING HAIR

Bahareh Farisabadi

Parched upon the ground, against a lasting sunset
With sunlight, hanging on a rope, neither to set
Nor rise
And its never-ending weary sway on the horizon
Whatever harbingering twilight
By it, is erased
Is blinded
Is buried.
The morgue and lockup and lane, all juxtaposed in
    an undying nightmare
And the martyrs of an undying revolution on
    fast-forward
Sealed onto every pendulum's to-and-fro over
    the lampposts
On the city veins intertwined
And on the ashes kept afloat over the cities.

As oscillates the rope, martyr is redefined
Grown tall
Shrunk short
Turned green, in its last swing, its brilliant face
    forever young
The face of kids content with eyes still glowing
    in their sockets.

As you turn your head
The indecisive solar pendulum
Kids' faces, forcefully pasted onto a tree
The comfort brought about by horror, torture,
    and humiliation

The tree; stains on a sad community life
Gallows set prepared in sunset landscape
And pure decorative oxygen.
As you turn your head,
The accelerating rope
The mix of prismatic colours; black and red and red and
    black and red and black
Thrown onto the pitted murder scene
And many-coloured backdrop of grace buried in the
    eternal bewilderment of your eyes
My fair tree-gallows land
The sunset coterie
Prismatic burial site
Chances that you laugh eternally; fixing a plant's pistil.
The agonising garden of hurts
A salve to mend your wounds
Gripped by female guilt-infested heredity
As if some rage you planted once in hallow soil.
The land of hair-gallowing Eves[1]
With breasts and thighs and waterfall hair, interlocked
The forged pose of heaven highs
Whose contumacious Eve, at last,
Avenges the Devil over her Fall
By snitching the dead sun
Into the effigy of everlasting inferno.

[1] In the biblical sense of the name.

ALONG THE NIGHT[1]
Bahareh Rezayi

Sleeting,
Flared up
In my voice.
Since Rabia time onward,[2]
I've been only adjacent to the night.
I hymn
And advance
And night
A black pencil
In my hands.

Adjacent to windy catch-phrases
I keep hooting
At my own image
And advance.
And become adjacent
To a terrain eclipsed.

Straight off with this very gaze
As I cave in
I set off into the night
And darker days
That comb the week's short hair.

I'm fasting most of the time these days
Successive silent fasting
And taste of wind
Hooting in my breaths.

I coil into myself
The world is cold, snowy.
Yet, I'm mindless of all
Within me, Rabia
Turns into a throat
And the snow, sitting on her hair
Is my hell.

---

[1] The title of this poem is an allusion to one of the most iconic, dark, and romantic films of pre-revolutionary Iranian cinema. Babak, who is afflicted with leukaemia, develops a romantic interest in a renowned singer named Parvaneh. She initially takes Babek for granted, but a relationship develops that changes both their lives.

[2] Rabia Balkhi (also known as Rabia al-Khuzdari) was a tenth-century poet who wrote in Farsi and Arabic. She is an important founding literary figure, being the first female poet known to have composed her verse in Farsi.

IT'S ALWAYS ABOUT A BIRD
Banafsheh Farisabadi

If we take it to be a bird
If we open its heavy wings wide with two indecisive
    thumbs
Heavy circles engaged, you could say night blind,
Where should they be suspended to flesh out death?
If the lid be a bird
At how in gapped intervals it'd better take off,
So that its sit-down on city cables
Becomes clear in perfectly rhymed elegies?

– You could say, myna –[1]

Take its body a Meybod dovecot[2]
The earth, opening its mouth wide
Rosewater washes its white-nape chicks off into
    the gutter
Death chant cooing pigeon seeds
Resting the case of its irreversible flight?

– Her old late highness –

Let's say the specks on that face a sandpiper
Cause of death: eve-time divagations at
    Kaleybar hillsides[3]
Her bizarre figure squatting on the bed
Even if as a swan's ogee curve in wetlands
Cause of death, solitary
Her fingers beaked off

Even if we say by a hummingbird
Cause of death: unidentifiable
Her head, say, a woodpecker
Whose cause of death we assume identified
To take the piebald legs she had
As estranged names for birds
In Tropic of Cancer
Wrap it in a death certificate
Cause of death: advancing where one shouldn't.

But if we take heart a bird
Then say parrot
Its tongue, that of seagulls
Its mute flight over all smiles in remembrance pictures
In swallows' tongue, departing to return every spring
In crew's time, always there
Burying her into the earth
As dictates the day.

And if we take the earth a bird
How far off the ground
My matchless oak was snatched
That now causes of death
Be clearly transcribed in pertinent documents?

[1] Written and pronounced similarly in Farsi and English, "myna" birds can be taught to speak. They often play a symbolically important role in the classical literature of Iran.

[2] The magnificent two storey Meybod dovecote was built to house nearly four thousand birds. It lies close to the ancient Naryn Castle, in the city of Meybod in central Iran.

[3] Kaleybar, close to the border with Azerbaijan, has a rich history. The city is renowned for its pigeon breeding and the architecturally unique structures built to house them.

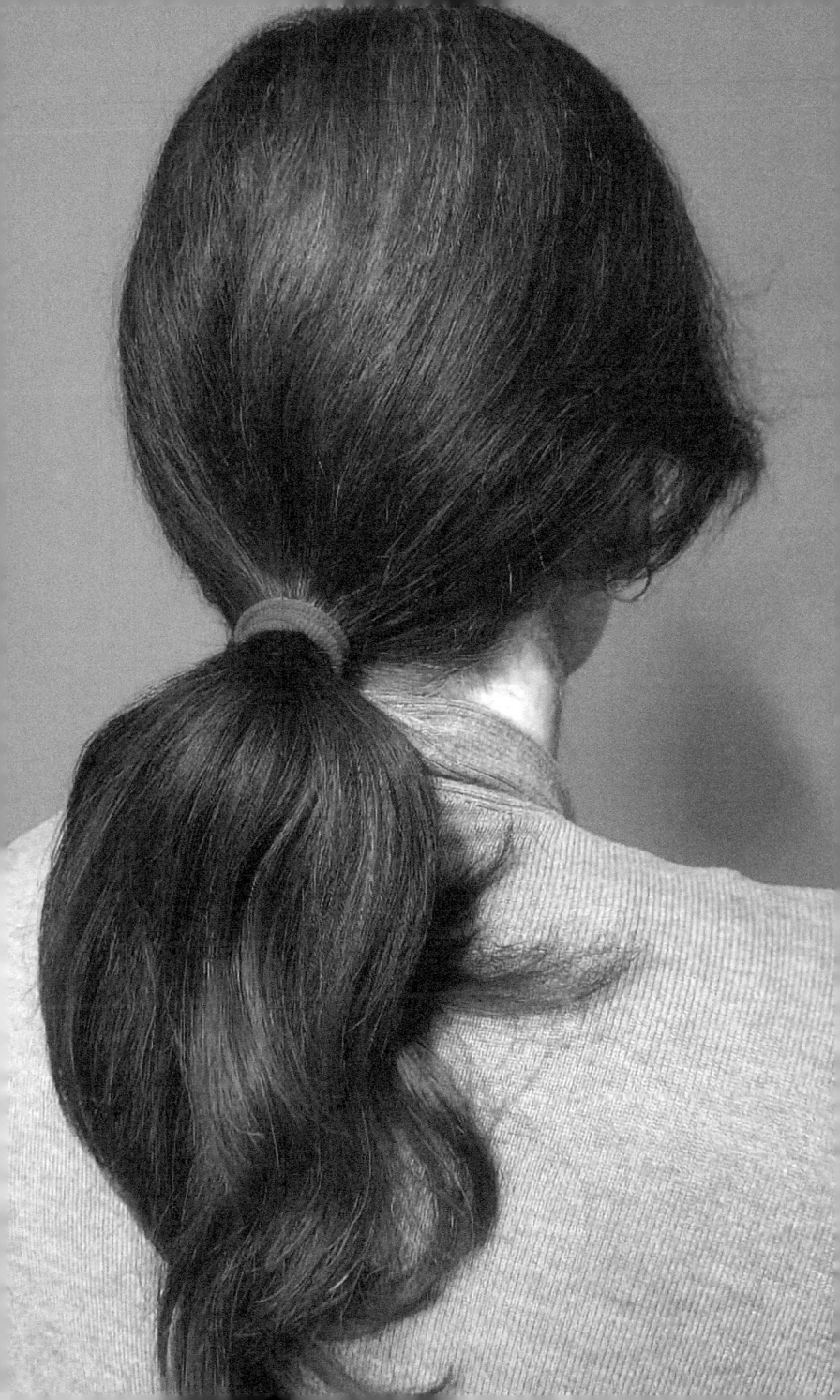

JÎNA[1]

Bita Malakouti

Author's note: Composed on the dark night of 19 September 2022.

Jîna!
You are the day,
Morning,
Earth, water,
The very tonality from depths of the night
Grains of wheat
Sprouted on a well mouth
Taste of blood, you are
On body outlines
Jîna!
You are the body
The eye
Ritual, motherland
Vein, window
The very elegiac call of Tahmineh[2]
The dread in motherly lullaby, you are
From her stapled lips
Jîna!
You are the gown,
The landing,
The ending, sleeping chamber
The bone, death
The red lane of that girl
Singing but dead
Dead but with showering hair
Jîna!
A mirror, you are
A mirror
Before the street
The river

Freedom
You are a path
Womanly wrath
You are a brook
The mother of Mercy
The waving banner
The very skirt
Gone with the wind
And on rooftops, all
Cedars abound.

[1] The name Mahsa is Jîna in the Kurdish language. This poem speaks of Mahsa Amini – murdered by the so-called morality police in Tehran on 16 September 2022. Her death sparked the Woman Life Freedom protest movement.

[2] Tahmineh is a character in the story "Rostam and Sohrab", part of the tenth-century Iranian epic, *Shahnameh* (The Book of Kings). Tahmineh is the royal daughter of Samanganshah, the king of Samangan. The novel depicts her as the infrequent lover of Rostam. Tahmineh gives birth to an illegitimate son: Sohrab. Unknown to Rostam, Sohrab is raised by his mother. The son matures into an exceptional hero and warrior, and during a decisive battle for Iran, he encounters his father in combat. Rostam kills Sohrab, and then discovers his filial connection to him. This poem draws a parallel between Tahmineh's lament for her son and contemporary Iranian mothers seeking justice for their children killed during the Woman Life Freedom protests. Mahsa Amini's mother is one of these women in modern-day Iran.

I AM SATIATED
Elham Gordi

Author's note: Composed between November–December, 2010.

I am satiated
With a tea
A woman once
Walked on,
With staggering steps
From a sack that seared the farm
And from a Bourgeoisie
That has adopted a local tone

I am lying down
In the north of this cup
And in the south, a worker
Winds sugar canes
Shred after shred
My mouth is sweetened
And sweet is the blood
Spilled in protest marches
Groping as it walks
Up to the university
Up to my scarf
Up to the morality that polices my hair
I've confessed
To green wristbands
To my sister's cure
In the mental hospital
Having turned her back to life
Taking selfies
I've confessed
To depression
To national festivals,

Where natal hymns are sung
And in the grand republic
Where enlightened minds
Are barricading the way
To plane trees felled
To urban cleaners
And Tehran, with its ruby necklace
Raise the curtain
Let me see the town
And the enchained statue
In the middle of the square
And a hanging cane
Who enjoys, much more,
The company of the dead.

I SAY MY NAME ON A BED OF ROSES
Elham Isapour

I say my name through the vaginal void of the word
When the radius of my tongue
Was thickened in a phallic circle of demise
And it was as if I had been whispering my own
    death chant
I say my name on vultures' rising necks,
Amidst a red word's throat
I say my name in the last puff
By a death-row inmate
When the millennial suns rise from gun barrels
And gunpowder moistens
In the eternal cold
I say my name on a rose-bed
Before those boys castrated in the slaughterhouse
Put a machine gun on mouthed death
I say my name through the vaginal void of the word
Before the ribbing echo of toads
Washes down the cannon booms
And by bats, torn apart
The phoenix in its nymph
I say my name in the last post-coital sigh
Let out by the Whore of Babylon[1]
In a hearse procession
Blessed by the grave
I say my name through the vaginal void of the word
Where the dying autumnal leaves
Where the howls of the silver hunting dogs
Sanction the winter
I say my name, before
The execution headcount
Nails the body
Onto a cross.

[1] The Whore of Babylon, as mentioned in the Book of Revelation of the New Testament, is associated with the seven-headed and ten-horned Beast of Revelation. "Idolatress" is perhaps a metaphorical translation of the Whore – who was prophesied to face destruction through her encounter with the Beast.

ATI…?[1] (abridged)
Ensiyeh Akbari

How far can one's body go on a self-hunting spree, leaving you behind, one after the other, once the blood, once bones, once mind, once heart, and even the skin, put you on the ground, corroding, hung on a rope? Answer me, Ati, I got nothing to put on… Ati…? There is this woman, fallen on my shoulders, with cast-iron arms; making words splash onto my face through her grinding locked rows of teeth, what have you done to yourself? And her voice, echoed in my head, as if I'd stood against a meaty sinewy mountain of oblivion, and the voice's echo smelling like shit. What have you done to yourself…? I carried the weight of despair, humiliation; the weight of barbed wire in vagina, in throat, in turbulence, in yuk, in gum, and even a tattoo of agony needling the clavicle; rusty all over. I have carried my dead mother everywhere throughout this last year; even in sleep, in anxiety, in nightmare, and before long, scorpions will stream out of ears, on my loin to kiss my mum, Ati. Check this catheter probing into my bullet-torn flank. Check the blood overflowing from the pipe sucking in the entire bed. Why though does everybody think the deep hole between our breasts, the one now turned into a bleeding acidic trench, is naturally born? I never answered that woman, Ati, I'm saying all this only to you… they said your bony shoulders were that of a dog's hips; and your stretched long hysterical laughter makes the massive sewage rats tremble; is it true? I still call you euphoria or serendipity, even when I could skip through you, on foot, on soles, as if a meaty catheter, from throat to anus, so that you could admit nothing flows within you but rolled dung dissolved in acidic muck. So then you'd reply, "Yes, yes, of course it is true! I am rolled dung balls with a ghastly ghost gasped into them, a ghost, trivial, obscene, fluorescent-driven, with a respiration that is the lover of yours! A well-arrayed army of tightly woven insects, with a human body, a mix of tentacles, feathers and microbes." When you had to wait for me to ripen up in the morgue, you said, when your body and face had gone through the cold, you said, "Ati, how does it feel to see the world through the eyes of a headless quail? Or through the eyes of an ant with half of its body dissolved in the bathroom's acidic detergent?" Fear, Ati... Fear people, fear the soil, fear the trees... a fear that transforms you into an orange carrot, inhumed into the earth's anus... in all the dark holes of this world left removed, unused. Being placed, placed, placed in the anus of therapy; in circles I draw in the air with fingertips, to then run around them for weeks or even months, say, a hamster in a running wheel in a terrarium. Fear! Fear the headless sheep behind the butcher's shop window. Fear and carry the madness on insanely like the softly ripening persimmons. Fear! The half-hidden excrement in the rice bag. Fear the grudge hidden in the watermelon, in kiwi. Fear the low-calorie oil, Ati. Fear the innocent beautiful feminine names... Fear the dawn, Ati!

[1] With the poet's permission, this poem was shortened and reformatted as poetic prose for reasons of space in this anthology.

YOU'D SAID…
Fanous Bahadorvand

You'd said
Don't write poems
Be a woman
Then life itself becomes poetic
Becomes spring
Becomes plain yet vivid
On the flow of wine in Mahsa's hair[1]
Or the nightly hair of Leily[2]
Free of whatever metaphor
Yet, I was the last resort
To words in ashes
In the hearty texts in flames
Or marble dead souls
Growing ever colder
Ice-ageing the world
And the landscape of my imagination
As if a gloomy sunset,
Expired on seven
In the morgues of paradise
The words in ashes
Were about to show
Death for life
And life for a persistent conspiracy
With ups and downs in a foe's synecdoche
Or certain self-decided deaths
But I was forced
To become a choice
For the heart
Poetry
"Woman
Life
Freedom…"

[1] Mahsa Amini, the young woman whose death inspired the Woman Life Freedom movement. She was killed in Tehran by the so-called morality police, on 16 September 2022, for showing too much hair.

[2] A common female name in Iran, but also a possible allusion to Leili in Nezami Ganjavi's epic romance, *Leili and Majnoon* (Leyla and Majnun in English). This book is often referred to as the Middle Eastern *Romeo and Juliet*, but Nezami's masterpiece was written in 1192, around four hundred years before Shakespeare wrote his play with a similar plot.

DO YOU RECALL PLAYING WITH MY HAIR?
Fariba Fayyazi

So it is
That the yellow column, parallel to the columnar
    backbones
Downtrodden
Far away from the words
The brain's hanging,
The heart, closed from within
The words once mine reckon me no longer
The nights
The moon
Light's yellow
Fever conquering my organs, spirally, life-sized,
As fog that proceeds and advances not
So it is
Waiting for the aquamarine clouds to rain blood,
    suckling on
One's own finger ad infinitum,
In commuting around the emergency zone
The lined up yellow columns thus are crushed in my
    backbones
My head in parallel with the cheeks
When one cannot wait to go, but cannot bear being away,
    in turmoil by fever
The night
The moonlight
A moth exiled from the light
From the day
Retreating into the night, into the restless swinging of
    one's head over a barely hanging neck
What's seen by the eye itself is incapable of seeing

The eyes left staring at the ceiling
Only the evident, the epiphanies beyond reach
My corpse's dispersion until it turns into a child,
    run me over, gather up, suckle the milk, so that I grow
In that I grow not until it is sated, and it is only the night
    that lets the juicy nectar keep running
Only the night
The moon
And the moonlight
And a cemented sky never having scented neither cloud
    nor blood
A cemented sky preoccupied merely with a pair of eyes
    obsessed with the ceiling
I steal the staring pair from the ceiling, and let the
    night shoot through the cement, the open cracks on
    the cemented night and meat, and blast the night of
    staring behind, so that the night shoots through the
    skin, and scatters veins and blood all over the meat, so
    that the night emerges, penetrating, in all its
    generosity, until sunrise, go to sleep in a single bed,
    burning the candles, raise, in all generosity, raise and
    bed not, so that the night is let in, to eat the heart that
    goes out, to gauge my gloominess out of my chest and
    blow into the golden face of death, who burns along
    with the candles, and laughs at the dark halves.
In the end,
The night gets up and leaves without shutting the door
    forever
The night becomes the day
Becoming it as if never before
Bruise streaks, of a night not existing from before,
    downpours filling the empty space in
The empty space is hollowed and re-filled
The sky drags itself lower and dissolves in flesh as
    disappearing down the drain
To that becoming becomes,
As it becomes trembling

CONT'D OVERLEAF   103

Which so happens and interlocked
So much so that
He flows in my veins
I am alone in his veins that exhausted death by their
    laughter in my veins, in my blood-free veins
The sad night that is a lost cause
Saddened by a bruise, a hidden line, to me,
    his reminiscence
Before I, ever have been written for him
So it is
That words escape from my grasp
I struggle to recognise a word
Thrown down from the sky, busy in the cellar
In an absolute lack of free will
I have lexically wetted myself from head to toe
So it is that
There will be no more morning prayer and the sun
    seemingly is setting

THE STANDING FIGURINE

Fariba Hamzeyi

There, the boulevard
At whose turn
You were standing
With your basic urge for makeup
Covered in mascara
Dripping down from your eyes
In a politically teary gesture
At the time of a wounded flank
No bird took flight
Into the chaos of your hair
And voice was committed to the throat
With those red lips that wouldn't dare
Tasting the words
With that disobedience
Ascribed to Neda[1]
With a bruise mark
Beneath chador[2]
Luring the ear
Into closet:
"So, there you are Maryam!"
In stupefied words by Atefeh
While underlining chaos
In your wounds
Where does your chaos lead to?
The same wind
At whose turn
You were standing
Letters showering from your hair
With no bird to flap wings
In honour of such showering

You were salvaged
In a grand charge
To that chaste temerity
In the boulevard's happening
When fairy-hair was a scene to behold
When comes the science of bruises
By the semen in the wind
Tu-whit! Tu-whoo!
That prophet of letter
Who were to practise metaphors
From that reddened mouth
Is standing, with his fists tight,
Amidst suicidal words
A summary enclosed into the azure
You can put on rouge to wash it down
Snatched from Neda's purse
Wrap chador round Atefeh's wit
As Maryam suffers
From ever more obsolete pangs
She who wanted to know
And did know where
To find sorrow in herself
And no matter from what angle
You expose Ra'na to it
It is still the same showering down.

[1] The Farsi female names appearing from here down through the poem – Neda, Maryam, Atefeh and Ra'na – are most probably of special personal significance to the author. The names eloquently illustrate the day-to-day suppression and discrimination that Iranian women have had to endure through the ages, and still do.

[2] *Chador* is a word that has found its way into the English language from Farsi. It refers to a long piece of cloth traditionally worn by Iranian Muslim women. The cloth covers the body from the hair down, leaving the face exposed but framed in colourful patterns. This lively traditional garment stands in stark contrast to the now more common, dour black version, which has been relentlessly promoted by the Iranian regime for over four decades since the 1979 Revolution.

AND THEN THE DESERT...
Fariba Sedighim

A drop of blood
Dripped down on the night
From the moon's finger, cut open
You never came!
The young seaweeds, drown in dead water
And you didn't come!
The sea covered your voice
And then the desert
Threw a handful of dust
Into the rain's eye

You grew old
Your thigh-high socks grew shorter
And the street grew shorter beneath your feet

Where is a swing
To help you raise your hands
And tickle the skies

And now you grow risks
Instead of plants;
Out of play,
A flag is jumping rope on your eyelids
Out of play,
A little boat carries your eyes afar
Out of play,
You hide behind a citrus tree with no seek

I'm sitting here, still
Looking at the ocean

That cries its inner turmoil
I'm sitting here
Gazing at this maths being done
And my fingers as lepers
And my hands
Suckled short by leprosy
You grew old
Your thigh-high socks still on the coat hanger
Dripping
When there was a shrill
Under the window's skin
Exposed to the wind

And behind glasses
Out of play,
The clouds had eyes
Swollen by cry

You grew old
And your mouth, opened in the form of a kiss
Came together, tight,
On the lips of death

DO CREATE
Farkhondeh Hajizadeh[1]

Author's dedication: To Khodanour.

Khodanour[2]
God of Light
God
God
God of Light
Why many a years
Weren't the letters in your name
Among the linearly confused lines of my deed?
Where found your footprint
Bare on deserted sands?
So that tears turn into grails
My Balouchi!
Your wish as if mine
How engraved your entire entirety
On my existence, my light-seeking existence.
Do create me anew!
Create me otherwise
Not in the suspended lines of an ID of no avail
That is engraved, the entire of your entirety
On my existence
And my existence as if yours
That is an air
Lit by your serenity, God of Light
Do create
You do create light
Create
Out of respect,
For the progeny of my tears
Multiplied
In the multiplication of the dark by the imposing God

[1] This poet and author (who is also the director of Vistar Publications) is the sister of Hamid Hajizadeh, a teacher and a poet from Kerman. On 22 September 1998, Hamid and his nine-year-old son were stabbed to death at their home. The Ministry of Intelligence of Iran never claimed responsibility for the killings. However, this heinous crime fits into a grand state-sponsored plan to eliminate an entire class of cultural figures – from Christian priests to Sunni clerics; from translators, poets, researchers, critics, intellectuals, and academics, to activists deemed a threat to the regime.

[2] Khodanour Lojjeyi, born on 2 October 1995, was wounded during the 2022 Zahedan massacre (known as Bloody Friday) by mercenaries working for the Islamic Republic of Iran. At least ninety-six protesters were killed and three hundred injured in Zahedan. Lojjeyi was taken to hospital, but died on what was his birthday after being prevented from undergoing surgery. Following his death – and after a photo of him was released showing his public humiliation and torture – Lojjeyi became one of the most iconic symbols of the struggle against the regime.

GIVING IN TO THE ORCHARD
Farnaz Jafarzadegan

We gave in
To the orchard blend
To a door
Tamed by the valley
To stones in a bed of blades
To the naivety of sickle and wheat
We were plucked
In the discursive maw
In speechless psalms
Flared up
The songs
And divinity rose
From the ashes
To burn the trees…
How then to grow green
From a bed of lies
A forest in remorse?

THUNDERBOLT

Farzaneh Ghavami

Author's note: Composed in September 2022.

Harken the magic of revolt in my insurgency
That made waters unstill
Harken the wanton thunderbolt in my eye
That placed a rainbow of gore on hands

An order delivered in me
From brains to heart
And the other way around
From cemetery to my bones
And the other way around

Leave me to the current spirits of water
Floating in the dark night
Running at daybreak
Leave me be with thirsty meadows

An order delivered in me
From knife to my hand
From hand to knife
From cry to my plea
From plea to cry

Leave me not to earth and decline
Leave me not to blood and dullness
Leave me instead to red flames and rage
While running in trip and trance
Floating in enflamed logs of ecstatic dance
Leave me to the windpipe burning from thirst

CONT'D OVERLEAF

An order delivered in me
From my blood to my mad
From mad to blood
From my cheer to vengeance
From my vengeance to cheer
Smothering, with a hundred blows
The one who turned my days dark as night
And my laughter lucid as tears
And my awake-ness nightmarish

Smother by an ending rage
The one who was, to me, the last twist of the knife
My towering child, by him, now in the grave
And my sigh spoiled since

An order delivered in me
From fear to my reverence
From revere to fear
From thunderbolt to my sky
From sky to my thunderbolt

Descend,
Do descend, O the thunder of dread and heart
'tis a long time
That I desire rain
Descend
Do descend, O the thunderbolt of lightning relief
'tis a long time
That I desire the end,
Then do descend.

ON FRIDAY, INSTEAD OF BIRTH CONTROL
Fatemeh Ekhtesari

On Friday, instead of birth control
Got kicked and punched around, heart-whole
On Saturday, instead of birth control
I said "No" and again the beating loophole.

I went to the middle of the street, fighting
Saturated by mythical blighting
I drank blood from my fractured nose
With birth controls, disinviting

I put lips on yours, laughing
Flooding from your body to the streets
Damned be these controlling pills
Damned be the prison locks, amassing

I feel within me, revived
A sense I left for years deprived
With shoes now running out of breath
I was to return to the path of no guide

In a grand scheme, all of us indeed
Should await beat-up and insult of it all
Yet the path runs in endless circles
As if on a carousel with no halt guaranteed

Although the heaven, heavy and choked
Weighing high on earth's shoulders
There is hope inseminated in my womb
I spew up a night that smoulders

CONT'D OVERLEAF

It might be akin to a miracle
Tasting blood with freedom savour
Perchance, again would shed hair
In us, a happy logic, plain and typical

There might be another fresher voice
In reply to the undying question, "If?"
On a Friday historically out of joint,
"Perhaps," but what endless grief

I'M A WOMAN
Fereshteh Eghbali

Fear me, as I become a woman
As I become of no man!
As a woman is freed in my mouth
As each finger of mine, a woman breaking the loop
As life bursts in me
As the kitchen, a shoulder
For me, to lay my head on
Fear me!
Fear me as I sweep
Every joint in my body,
My homeland,
As I become a siren
At the heart of the capital
Fear as every strand of my hair
Lock after lock loosens
At the end of the first person
As I become a woman
As I become of no man!
As I am a womanly dress in everyday pupils
As I become a knife to a womanly bone
Manning up in itself
Of no man
Am a woman
As sobs the womb mourning my femininity
Fear the murder of monthly foetuses
Warning you about this bleeding sorrow!
As go to decay the body every month
In an indecisive solitude
As I abandon my bodily plea
Fear not!

CONT'D OVERLEAF

As I have passed through you
As I am a woman!
And my body,
Ransomed over freedom
As I become a woman,
For life and freedom.
Fear the man,
As a woman starts lurking under his skin…

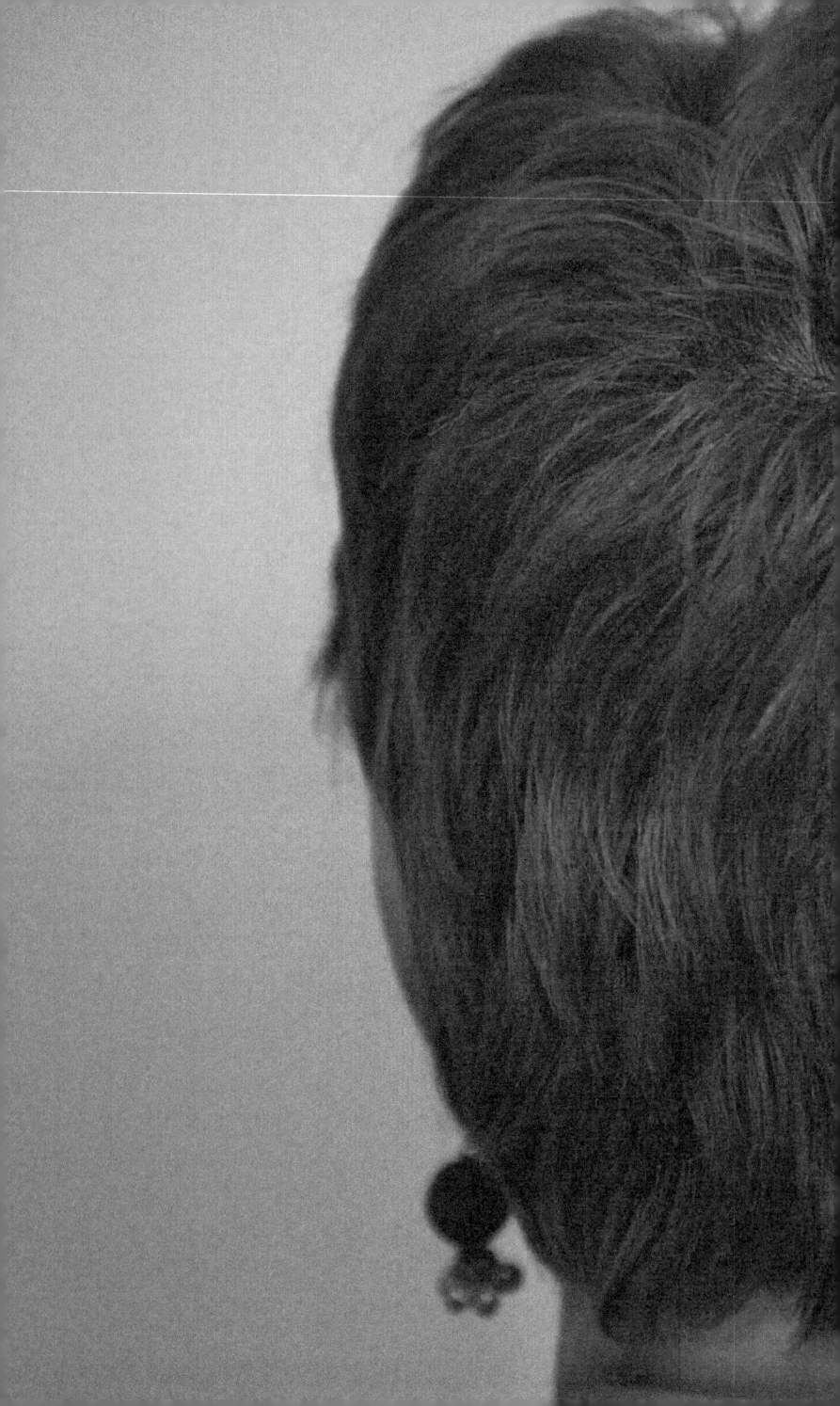

SHEHERAZADE[1]
Fereshteh Sari[2]

Sheherazade
For a thousand times and one
Leaves her story
Yet, can no more delay
Anyone's death
Danger
Is no more a king betrayed
Easily recognised

Sheherazade
Has got herself a new car
So that on highways
With breakneck speed
She chases the introverts
Of nested stories ever-new
And warns them of danger

Today
Already worn out by air pollution
Parks under a tree withered away
Hardly has she unfastened her seatbelt
Than a barefoot boy
Shows up with a bundle of papers in hand
He has no magic lamp
And Sheherazade tries
To force him into her car
And take him back to her story
So that he's saved
From giant genies released in the streets
The young Aladdin instead

Is only after selling papers
Done trying
Sheherazade
Turns on the car radio:
"Serial killing of prostitutes in Mashhad,
    seventeen so far..."[3]
Sheherazade
Is held up behind traffic lights
And murderers run away
Having recognised her,
And thus having followed her,
A reporter
Was fired
After reporting on Sheherazade's failed attempts
For a thousand times and one

[1] Sheherazade, a woman born to a noble family, is the main character
and storyteller in the classic *One Thousand and One Nights* stories.
She is imprisoned in the sleeping chamber of a psychopathic king,
who has promised to kill one virgin every day because his wife
betrayed him. Sheherazade delays her death by recounting stories,
with which she nightly entertains the king. After one thousand and one
nights she runs out of stories, but the king has already fallen in love
with her, and instead of executing Sheherazade he decides to marry
her. In this poem, Sheherazade appears in a contemporary urban
Iran, where she is faced with the horrifying news of women being
discriminated against today.

[2] Fereshteh Sari is one of the most esteemed contemporary Iranian
poets. She is also a translator, researcher, editor and writer, with
seventeen volumes of published work and multiple Iranian and foreign
literary awards to her name.

[3] Sheherazade's contemporary world includes the real-life serial
killer Saeed Hanaie. He was a forty-year-old builder who murdered
sixteen prostitutes in Mashhad, in northeastern Iran. Hanaie, who was
sentenced to death by hanging by Iran's Supreme Court, confessed to
killing the women, but said he was carrying out the "will of God".

WAITING FOR GODOT
Forough Sajadi

I lost you in streets and a future that inculcate
Non-sensible
Climbing the traffic lights,
In hope for a bird
Street after street
The city has palpitated in our alleyways
When the Emirates were ranting against the Gulf
And kids kick the ball over the grass
And cafés cramped by people like us,
A whole different class of human beings
And our hair, rows of suicidal firing lines
When Mahzad, the sweet child of the moon,
Cleaved the alleyway, carried it on shoulder
In search of some doable connection speed
Lest her employers cry not on Arabian models
When the wait wasn't just for Godot
And the street would go asymmetrical
Torn between hope and fear
You in there, I here
And this life is not normal
Never had been
As Helen is but a motive for the Trojan Horse
And, to us, a plane solely consisting in…

I lost you as I perceived myself through the eyes
    of the street
And the now gone dead-ended alleyway
Now it makes no difference who's climbing the wall
When the wall sets its balance right
In the continuity of a scaffold,

Where you are still hanged in my mind
And yet there's no originary for either fear or fear not
You in there, I here
Prison, only such that words climb its walls in riot
And Helen but sheer motive for horse-making
Trojan, tough, is now viral, connecting here and there.

COMING FROM THE OPPOSITE
Ghazaleh Zarrinzadeh

You come from the opposite
While daggering from behind
There the bruise, there the crack
The passage abandoned by the inner me
Where you were a bandit once
And cracks opened my heart
I am folded in two
Your wife
And my own husband
I'd been
Have become a man
My thin hands
And tired feet
Kicking at your life
I've become a man
And it was the woman
I stitched
To the flimsy bee pin
On your shirt.

A CONVERSATION
Hengameh Hoveyda

Haven't told you
We have unshareable memories
There is a door in hell
Opening to a pair of nightmare-impregnated eyes

All the awe
Yet of no history, abridged or unabridged…
And the burn wouldn't go this deep
If only we had forgotten not
That all infernal doors
Find their way
To a body among ours.

What do you have to say to those who rise dancing
    as fire whispers?

One day we will mourn
The river course through and through
From the heights of your eyes to the furthest depths of
    an earth as its bedrock

One day, and for all who mourn in cradles
For the day they grow tall
And rise…
To win their names over again
And the sun defies
Being thrown back into the sky
Holding its ground
Beating out standing!
A crushed cigarette butt on the asphalt

CONT'D OVERLEAF   129

You kick it to the side with the tip of your shoe
Telling yourself
I'm from this hell…
The hell with where I'm from!
I have my own memories, perhaps
And names, and mourning…
Born in the mirror
And buried in it
There are many mirrors
That I have to carry on my shoulder
Illumination is just to forget…
I am turning the lights off, one after the other
These infernal lights

THE UNTIMED
Jamileh Jalilzadeh

I go obsolete
In the lexicon of the day
Am related somehow
To wine and sea
Related though doubtfully
To poems untimed
Strangely related to mothers
In a midday with no day in its middle
An unrelenting amnesia
Rendering me suspicious

A missing first person, I become
With the missing of my own
So that we give birth
To naked words.

I CARRY THE SILENCE
Katayoun Rizkharrati

They'd aimed their guns
At us
Among us, someone cried "death"
And her voice echoes in all mouths
They're looking at me
At the flag on my skirt, torn apart
At the world under my steps,
At my skin, growing dark.
I was ready to fight
Walking backward.
From hares only left
A handful of pink bones
From my sister
A woman who hid her beauties.

I was turning back
With someone's cry: "death"
And then woke up the orchard;
You can't summon the sadness lost in history,
Can't dance so much
That your skirt turns into a flag
And seasoned soldiers return home.

On the way to the river, I count the lights
The abandoned shoes,
As if looking for you.

Looking for a street
Returning to the city's heart
So that it pumps blood into all streets

Bullets passing right next to our ears
I fail to find you
In morgues
In cemeteries
In street corner trenches
You aren't behind AK-47s

I move about the garbage in my town
Silently
And wander about in streets unarmed
I carry the silence weapon-free,
And think of you even as I die.

Fear passes through the eye of a needle
So do batons
I cry for my sister, getting to the dorm late
Buses are set on fire
So are city bins
And streets furnished with a shredded war

Your skin enflamed in street fire;
As if ignited blood splashed on asphalts
Looking at me
At my skirt, that now is a flag
And my mouth, aiming at them with silence

TO BECOME A GRAVEYARD PIECE
Leila Hekmatnia

To sit me down, for wings
Of untaken flights
To position my eyes on a face
Of proportions with a beauty
Millennially afar
To tell me of listening to a moment
When you've detoxified the story
Supportless, exposed
How to become a tree without sitting in soil?
How could things grow in this climate for the time
   of need?
Look! In the crunch of blockaded paths, not by snow,
   but by blood… in the crunch of such paths,
   I was becoming a midwife
And pregnant was a woman who gutted herself out and
   became the Trojan horse for this city
They still recognise me alive, as "being one of them,"
   making my lips and hands unwanted
Is it still me, the living witness of this crowd with their
   iconic fabricated bruises?
Siege me as, in my dreams, I was wild awake
   for whatever sound three nights in a row
Three nights in a row, I dreamt being left alone,
   a loneliness of staring eyes never turning away
Three nights in a row I dreamt of what a pain in vain
   to part with your body
Three nights in a row, I dreamt he who brought shiver
   and thunder on us, now antedates death in exchange
   for a grave shared between us

Yet, the awakening morning impregnated my hands
    with a sun legitimised to cross through the warmth
    of blood
In my living body parts a voice remained muffled by
    ceaseless rant
The earth turned into an encasement fermenting us
And God into one laying worms in my layers of hurt
I am made to run again under charged clouds, as the
    rain in the sky, they are raining all over my skin:
    bless you!
This is their moment, spoil it… spoil it when blood
    fails to impact
The most abysmal impudence of town, my mouth,
    if it vibrates
Ask how all this would gather in me?
How foot-bathed and red-lettered, at the same time?
In faces I reckoned being left alone by he who knew
    the crowd's language
Ask the crowd, how would I unshoulder the mountain
    on the ground?

FREEDOMINANCE
Leila Sadeghi

You were born, as was the world by me
You were born, as was planted the earth by me
You were born, as was killed time by me

Your birth site, Jîna,[1]
You were to be born to endow life
For wherever was I unborn

Woman, said I[2]
In a house of my element
Freedom, said I
Lo! You, she who splashed her hair against
   the moonlight
Generations whirl in your repeated blood

Horses hoofing in a millennial siege
Forever freedominating, for ever freedominance
Tell of the long showering hair as I rise against
   your death
Tell of the historiest passage to all the blood shed
   in its name
Of the girl fiddlesticking bone on hair
A soldier buried under a gravestone decorated by
   his mother
A girl dreaming to reverse gravity by studying physics
The same gravity they say made a petit excuse for your
   free-fall
I stand here, stone to conjugate freedominance
The ones I desire not standing before me, gun in hand
In a world where to give birth is conjugated by death

Histories spilled over stories dialogue-adverse
A say bothered with no hear, that of the Divine!
And this prison beyond a mere word
Name of a woman who died giving life
With her hair, naming people anew
A new phrase repeated by many, heard by a few
Where Liberty is but a busy square[3]
And no one knows whose name they coin
To assert the streets

In whose name, you are battered while falling and why
Where life is conjugated given and taken, equivocally
Conjugating the world, in word, old as is the human age
To get a scent of it
To behold, even if only for once
Draw your breath! As to win and lose, obverse sides
    of the same coin

Nothing worth drawing but this very breath
Nothing worthier than releasing a breath withheld
As you press a knee against my throat
Step off, let me draw breath, saying
Freedominance, freedomination, to behold, for once,
    unconjugated

[1] Mahsa Amini (also known as Jîna Amini) was a 22-year-old Kurdish-Iranian woman. She was arrested and killed by the regime's so-called morality police on 16 September 2022. Her death resulted in the rise of the Woman Life Freedom protest movement.

[2] This is a poetic expansion on the Woman Life Freedom slogan.

[3] This refers to a historical square in Tehran. It was previously named Shahyad Square, before being renamed Liberty (Azadi) Square in honour of the 1979 Iranian Revolution.

AN ELEGY ON THE EARTHLY DAUGHTER
Leili Galehdaran

Author's note: Composed between August–September, 2022.

O, daughter of the earth
O, earthly daughter
O, pure asterisk girl of the earth
O, O, O, the earth, O earth, O earth
O, the earth!
Still a child, your maturity
Not yet exhausted much
Lay your hand on broken head
But raise your head
And see that sky too has a broken head.

O, beauty of the earth
The basement gets what it is to be chaste
Don't fret, don't sweat
They don't spill virgin blood in there
There the festive muses are those of rage
Gowns torn, grails broken, hair plucked
The empyrean heaven trembles
Not by unveiling your hair,
But your cry of despair
History's virgin, to and fro,
Back to back
To back this grievance for vendetta

O earth, O earth, O, O, O, arise
From the earth, you, the mother,
Cut her shroud as high as her stature
Measure her maroon waistcoat
Along with a larger pair of sandals
And, for God's sake, this time pack her bundle

With no haste.
In the world,
Six feet under,
She still grows taller,
Older,
Bigger,
Taller
Than you
Than all.

THE REEDS

Mahin Khadivi

Author's note: Composed in Atlanta, Georgia,
between October–November, 2019.

Dear Mr Shakespeare
You, missed dearly these days
Redo your song
Forget tragedy

***

Girls lost
Boys in blood

The city in mourning
And in mourning, mothers
Hamlet, dead

***

Reeds on fire
Fish decapitated
Koureh ignited[1]
Fridays dragged in here with both hands cut off
No rider was there, palanquins spoiled.
Mothers tearing blood
Girls hung with their own scarves
Hassan's groom suit put on a straw man
Dear Mr Shakespeare
They aimed with machine guns
Yaghoub's eyes collapsed into the fish mouth
Forget the sword
It is a different story, the mourning that goes on
    in this bleeding land

***

Dear Mr Shakespeare
You are missed so dearly these days
When tragedy
Is limitlessly
Catastrophic

***

The reeds are green no more
Nor yellow
They have become blood-soaked
I can't go to sleep
Mr Shakespeare
Forget about Othello
Desdemona is decimated now.

[1] Impoverished neighbourhoods around Mahshahr, near the Persian Gulf, where local protesters were massacred by the regime during nationwide protests in 2019. The names Hassan and Yaghoub that appear in this poem honour the memory of two such martyred protesters.

ZAHEDAN[1]
Mandana Zandiyan

It's called Zahedan
The captain of its own wounds, in blood.
Agony is bifurcated in the humidity of her eyes
As she blinks each time
And death aches
By the discriminatory sermon,
Boiling out in the bullet's throat, tall and
Gasped out of life,
In epitaph-free graves.
It's called Zahedan
And light
Passing through her veins,
Solemnly, made bass,
White,
Swayed in the call of the street,
Which unfolds,
Singing,
Dancing to the song,
"Death to the dictator!"[2]
Echoes in history's voice and
Human throat.
On which side of silence does
The world stand
That its hands
Cannot reach agony's forehead?
With complacency,
Not shed from its shoulders,
Not standing in pause,
Before the mirror, head-on,
Becoming rage, thunder, and fire?

Which part of voice has collapsed,
That this full eclipse knows no passing?
Doesn't see, doesn't hear:
It's called Iran
And that wretched femicide
That has chained to itself death,
Doesn't know
Life is making love to freedom
And the poetry of all the living
Called Mahsa.[3]

[1] The poem elegiacally references the Zahedan massacre, also known as Bloody Friday, during which almost one hundred people died or disappeared, with three hundred injured. The series of violent crackdowns against protesters, who had gathered to chant outside a police station near the Great Mosalla of Zahedan, began on 30 September 2022.

[2] This was one of the protesters' key slogans at Zahedan. It is also currently shouted during Woman Life Freedom demonstrations. Since 2009, the slogan has been directed at the Supreme Leader, Seyyed Ali Hosseini Khamenei. Khamenei came to power in 1989, and is Iran's second Supreme Leader since the 1979 Iranian Revolution.

[3] Mahsa Amini, who was murdered by the so-called morality police in Tehran on 16 September 2022, and whose death triggered the Woman Life Freedom protest movement.

IN SPRING

Manoureh Ashrafi

In spring
I hide
As if an offshoot
In dark earth,
In rain
I hide
As if a cracked land

In love
I hide
As if a soul
In awakeness
Submerged
In constant labour
Yearning to grow
Blossom
And sprout.

THE ORANGE DRESS

Maryam Hosseinzadeh

Author's note: Composed between April–May, 2010.

You, the orange dress I failed to put on
Or else, to take to my ruins for sale
Or to the neighbour's corner-lot butchery
At that crossroad with a winking red light
And that unaccounted-for orange vendor
Then do count
How many mes are subtracted[1]
Every single day, one of mes, put against the wall
War declaration all across the chambers in my head
And my home wholly mortgaged to madness
You, red dresses
Toy with my dark pimples
Pick a half of my angel-free wings
Leave the twin halves of its remaining ashes behind
Pick them all
We are not meant to return home
   with ever-empty hands
And our half-wishes left orphans
Thus, harken my midnight prayers

Lo, thou, the cynosure that grants all wishes
Fulfil the wish of a hand torn apart
To my sleeves cut off
Do grant
To grant
To let me wear back the un-black
To furbish up blisters on my clothes
Under my body's skin
Do grant
To grant

CONT'D OVERLEAF

That I burn wild rues
Every day to protect sunlight,
Oh Lord! Against the ominous eyes[2]
Against bruises in disguise

Be fended off and off
I thus do blow
At all those rooms in relationship with you
And its walls,
God forbid, would ever recognise me all in black.

[1] Translator's note: In Farsi, the poet uses "me" in the plural; hence in this and the following line I have translated it as "mes".

[2] This alludes to an old but enduring superstition in Iran about the negative impact of certain people's gaze – especially if met while they are paying someone a compliment.

GOWHAR ESHGHI[1]
Maryam Jafari Azarmani

In the name of Gowhar Eshghi, of woman,
  a name all of fame
The poem in hand commences by mourning
  our motherland in flame

Scarf, chador, dress, you are mourning head to toe
Motherland is you yourself pain-conquered, to and fro

Your earth, memories, bleeding by madness
Maddened by blood your mirrored sigh of sadness

In honour of the slaughtered young like your son, Sattar
Of the spite amassed in throats, of torn strings on guitar

Even if deceitful horns of tyranny play out
  scream loudest
It is your bruised voice that proves relentlessly proudest

How wretched weapons in their fear of you
How wretched the wretched in all their ado

But in the heart of all this chaos and dark
And against this collapsed era, the last spark

And so Mother became the name chosen by all the free
And Woman turned victorious in her struggle
  for equality.

[1] Gowhar Eshghi is a civil rights advocate and one of the so-called Iranian "Justice-seeking Mothers". Any woman in Iran who has lost a child since the 1980s and is seeking answers from the state about is referred to as one of these mothers. Gowhar is the mother of Sattar Beheshti, who is mentioned in this poem. Sattar was an Iranian blogger, killed in November 2012 after being tortured while in the custody of the Islamic Republic's security forces. After his death, Gowhar Eshghi made many attempts to bring her son's killers to justice – but to no avail. Despite her advanced age, Eshghi has been subjected to physical assault and injury by plain-clothes security personnel working for the state. In 2022, the BBC named her among the top one hundred most inspiring women in the world.

TIME TO BECOME A WOMAN

Maryam Raisdana

Author's note: Composed on 14 January 2023.

I confess
To be a plant
On day one
The earth, drew my veins to itself, in sturdiness
A millennial palm, amidst the sandy terrains of Persis[1]
And I was fertilised with such lunar fruits
Time for me
To become a woman
A bold offshoot
And a walkway
Of a thousand grains

I am, now,
The sun brought sons into my bosom
And moonlight cultivated daughters in my hair

History's pages turn in dark and blood
Bodies violated
Hair is cut
Rage replaced life
Grudge replaced the eye
The multitude disenchanted,
Blood spattering the sun
And woman, condemned
As half-minded and half-shared
The vanguard of free life legends
With chivalrous hair, an army each strand
Dismantled the globe of ignorant madness
Now stone by stone
Mountain by mountain

The echo in the range is hers
Now, not drop by drop,
From the unremitting roar of rivers
To the sound of the sea
All hers

And beneath her feet
The storm
Is turning the page
Of history
Enamoured by freedom,
As the genesis of a plant
With a thousand and one roots
In a gripping fist.

[1] Greek for "Parsi" – Iran's ancient name, from where we get the modern rendition, Farsi.

IN MY THROAT'S PURGATORY
Marziyeh (Maryam) Bermal

In my throat's purgatory
Neither words, nor silence
A universe of lines
Given meaning, by our beholding
And the temples, full of guns.
Let me recollect you,
No words involved, with new austerities
Since words are doomed to un-living
And authorised to perish
Oh, brother! Only a handful of words
And the close of day
Don't epitomise yourself in prayers
Be the rain
Of the same long pregnant cloud
With probable drop of blood
From gun barrels
When the world is mandated to bullets
And amidst the windowpane
My hair, in a dancing flow
Which is
Unprecedented
In oaths made by memory
A dead-end within a desert
In my throat's purgatory...

THE CALL
Mona Zahedi

Turn about
In this hapless path
With these hands disseminated into agony
Rehearse the ritual of mirror in reflecting water
Since this death, formed the ring of our uprising[1]
Strings of hair, lashing out
Bruised shoulders.

Where sunlight furrowed
Through her hair
When the girl, put her hijab on a stick[2]
And rose to sky a flag gone pale
And when the self-immolated woman[3]
Was coaxed into a loud cry
In the runny madness of the city.

In the name of that woman who was burnt
Turned into ashes
Turned into dust
Gone with the wind
Sitting on our cheeks.

In the name of Woman, Life, Freedom
Echoing from spirit to spirit
Turning into a song
Into singing
That made the earth beneath insomniac.

NOTES: THE CALL (previous page)

[1] This refers to the death of Mahsa Amini on 16 September 2022.

[2] A reference to Vida Movahhed, a young Iranian woman who in December 2017 held her headscarf aloft on a stick while standing on a street utility box. Her protest against mandatory wearing of the hijab took place almost five years before Woman Life Freedom protests began.

[3] Homa Darabi (b. 1949) was an Iranian child psychiatrist, academic, and political activist affiliated with the Nation Party of Iran. Darabi is known for her self-immolation, as a result of which she died in 1994, in protest at the use of the hijab. Her act of self-sacrifice was among the earliest and most tragic of its kind.

A RUBBER BAND

Monireh Parvaresh

A rubber band
A few centimetres
I tie around my hair tight
Only an air shot for warning
And then I announce to the world:
"The war is over
Crawl back to your caves."

DEAR GOD
Nahid Arjouni

Dear great God
Occupying my kitchen too now
Reading my medications' labels
Please step back a little!
I need to rinse these dishes
And think of something to cook for lunch
As I'm talking to you
Nah, I'm fine, don't need any help!
I myself can tend to everything
The guest room needs sweeping
Lunch won't be overcooked
I'll answer the phone myself
And dust off this picture frame...
You recall?
Here I was so young
And you hadn't yet turned all furious back then
And I wasn't used to taking antidepressants
It was right after the taste of strawberries and sleep
When you started frowning
At my thirteen years of age
The sheets
And dreams
Sorry to put it bluntly
But your heart was set
For whatever I had in my pockets
My small purse
And even my lockable chest!
You, the great God sitting in my kitchen
I'm now an ideal woman
Nothing to hide in my pockets

My purse left open on the table
Taking my antidepressant QH8[1]
And I've promised my therapist not to have
   worrying thoughts
Please kindly raise your feet
It's time to mop.

[1] Q8H is the abbreviation for Quaque Octa Hora, a Latin medical
instruction meaning "every eight hours".

ARE WE DEAD OR ALIVE?
Nahid Kabiri

Being frail,
You cough
The notes of an end-of-autumn cold
Into a cloth
So that you conceal
Your five o'clock rendezvous
From the conspiracy
Of suspecting passers-by
Which street has broken
Your perfume;
Before you got to the turn of the alley
Which led you to no fond place
In dead-ending paths?
What were, after all, your share of petty joys in life
Other than a shopping basket
That would drag you to the market of nightingales,
    sunlight, and flowers,
With longing Kajol-lined eyes
And with an undecided smile
So that in the restless azure of alleys
Place a violet onto your hair
And ask,
In the voluminous presence of
Onions, rice and kitchen spices,
From the oven and tea pot,
Ey...
Are we dead
Or alive?
In fearsome cold seasons,
Love is an atonement
In cahoots with a girl next door

And her heart
And "they" tonsured her hair today
　and all the way through
Her mother, with rushing fingertips
Pried apart the entire pomegranate orchard,
From home to the wounded dripping alleyways
　to the streets;
And I
Both, admire the girl-next-door's hair
And the mirror,
Comb,
Café,
Ice cream,
And my hair untamed
To keep the flow
In a windy mid-east,
Till the night-time when
The cloud and
A few stars and
A block of sky
Shine on the table and curtain and an apple
Half-bitten, and the desolated room.

Wearier than days and dreams, the shadows
Crossing through red lights and the
　whistling traffic police
Lined to cry, "Down with the dictator"[1]
And yonder, a little dove
Puffing up its rain-soaking feathers
Against the leaden sunset
As dissolving crows, caw...

---

[1] "Down with the dictator!" and "Death to the dictator!" are common slogans shouted at Woman Life Freedom demonstrations. The "dictator" being the Supreme Leader (Ayatollah), Seyyed Ali Hosseini Khamenei, who came to power in 1989. He is Iran's second Supreme Leader since the 1979 Revolution; Ayatollah Khomeini, who famously issued a *fatwa* against the British author Salman Rushdie, was the first.

THE LORD OF THE BITTER PALM
Narges Doust

Hey you,
The sigh
The path
Remember branches
Spattering night
When was dead all lit
The God of the weary moon!

Hey you,
The God of branches all dead and dry
As hard-to-reach as that towering date-palm

It was you I desired!
Yet you
You were the God of Mullahs
Preaching from pulpits made of wood and stone
And not of the sorrow
Felt by innocent and woeful body branches
Originated from pinot noirs
Here, palm's suffering so deep
That, at times, I took the wind's visage
To the desert and brought the earth instead
I, at times, cried in naked waters.
Now, what difference to you, me sighing
When you are mute, as if a brute,
Gazing at Luna, unable to salute! [1]
Luna,
Who got killed
Under the south sun of rouge and noir

And catastrophic Tehran
Started to snow
Started to snow
Until Tehran collapsed.
The fever-spawn,
Bodily bleeding nonchalant

Sigh! Do you see
In the stature of night
Every nook and cranny of the carnal orb, or not?

Lo! The Big Bear Lord
No nook and cranny on stars

Has nothing to do with the mouth
On death
You must rise out of the gaffe
That revolts in the night

Like my both palms
Heading high in prayers
Knowing how incapable is
This aquatic benediction
Under the azure sky

Aye, aye, rush me not
To a salvation of a thorny rage,
The wind diminished in salvaged fleshly flowers
Sigh, it died!

Speaking of which, you, the moon,
Where are buried those of us gone?
Does this aquatic Lord
Know the secret
Behind the yellow nooks and white crannies,
Or not?

CONT'D OVERLEAF

No,
No,
While moaning, I recognised a sad palm,
Who crushed the Lord of all branches
As its forehead touched the earth!

[1] In Farsi, the name Leila is used in the poem here. Leila is a common female name in Iran, and one that always alludes in the nation's cultural imagination to Nezami Ganjavi's epic romance, *Leili and Majnoon* (Leyla and Majnun in English). The language-play in the poem around this Farsi name can be transposed to "luna", and the particular symbolic connotations of the moon in the English language and indeed universally: femininity, time, immortality, eternity and light as well as shadowy darkness.

I WENT ON STRIKE

Nastaran Makaremi

Author's note: Composed on 5 January 2023.

I went on strike 'cause I wanted to stay in bed
　　and see nobody's face.
I went on strike 'cause no matter how long I waited,
　　the day wouldn't break and clocks were frozen
　　in the night.
I went on strike 'cause I was well-fed in face of hunger,
　　the fashion of the day.
I went on strike 'cause I had hope in face of hopelessness,
　　being contingent.
I went on strike 'cause it was Tuesday with its portions
　　stinking like a chicken's ass.
I went on strike 'cause the air had wrinkles on it
　　and it was as if someone was blowing into my mouth
　　with a malodorous breath.
I went on strike 'cause certain words were such torture.
I was nauseated by all the "to his highness" and "yours
　　sincerely" and "with regard to" and "kindly note…"
I went on strike 'cause I went eve to eve in search of a
　　woman singing beneath my window once years back.
I went on strike 'cause bulky louses have come to life's
　　lasting elixir in our office.
I went on strike for that young student who asked me,
　　cold: "You think anything will change?" and snow
　　melting on his bright hair as if falling on the sun.
I went on strike for the night that was dripping ink,
　　devouring me the entire day.
I went on strike for light, screaming: "Nothing here
　　is permitted."

CONT'D OVERLEAF

I went on strike for the tired whores being washed off
     from their client's mind, burnished off, as if ageing
     dust, getting free stuff from familiar convenience
     stores.
I went on strike for a child I never had to piss
     on my dreams and keep kicking the wall in his room
     out of anxiety.
I went on strike for that woman, once standing on the
     bridge, spitting down at those passing by, who threw
     herself down once she noticed me, and spattered all
     around the ground like drools.
I went on strike for life in a land where life was so
     all-time low that all else felt fancy in comparison.
I went on strike 'cause freedom never chanted for me
     and passed by under my window, mute.

THE SINGING STONES
Nayyer Farzin

She wanted to keep the sky from falling
Yet they lapidated her hands
But what were they,
Other than a paper rolled into a crumble?
Even before her
Her dreams were seen by others
The blues of them censored
A good punishment for a woman
Delivering birds in hell
Her hair could
Be a dove's nest
Her hair
Lines in a poem
Deemed unpublishable

They had cut the birds' throats
And the woman was left teaching stones how to sing.

FOR YOU, THE CODE[1] (abridged)
Nazanin Ayghani

Darkish ringlets
Covering the air!

Pour down snow from bare skin
On dusk
On the purple jugular vein put to burn

On brutality
On a temple on fire…[2]

Wajiha![3]
Fair and young!
Darker than the wind!
Rise above the eye-sockets!
Be a deer over your carcass!

You, the oil-rich damned virgin!
On this darling's crown
This blood scared off lunar-ly
Lo the daggery meadow
Drizzling all over
Your veined-out breasts

You
The mother!
The drifting womb!
The lioness!
The land!

Rush into the eclipse[4]
You, death angel's youth!

Carry her aloft
Dropped on promiscuous soil
A tongue-twisting mourn
Over her dusted bridal chamber

On shoulders, do carry her
And put stone
Her body –
A sweet venom sting

All dreams, now
Broken
As is her corpse
Broken as it gets touched
By the alien washing hands[5]

Ablute her!
A dry ablution[6]
Of this blood
Of this shame
Of this fallen god…

NOTES: FOR YOU, THE CODE (previous pages)

[1] This poem is about Mahsa Amini, who was killed while in police custody. Her death ignited the Woman Life Freedom movement. The "code" of the poem's title refers to Mahsa's original tombstone, which was later vandalised by security forces or supporters of the regime. An inscription (in the Kurdish language) read: "Jîna [Mahsa in Farsi]: you won't die – your name will become a code." This idea was interpreted by an anonymous graphic designer in complex interwoven calligraphy spelling the words Woman Life Freedom (see the graphic on page seven). Much to the annoyance of the regime, activists at demonstrations substituted this graphic for the central motif on the Iranian flag – which is said to symbolise the Koranic declaration *Allah-o-Akbar* (God is Greater).

[2] Intended as a pun here. In translation, we can conflate an enflamed temple as a place of worship, with the temples at the sides of one's skull when impacted by a gunshot.

[3] A woman's name – from the Arabic – meaning both coy in appearance and having a beautiful face.

[4] An allusion to *Ghassal:* the washer of the dead during Islamic funeral rights.

[5] This alludes to the Arabic call for prayer, *Hayy-a ala al-Salat* (Hurry to Prayer) – with the last word changed to *khosouf*, meaning eclipse.

[6] The word used in the original text is the Arabic, *Tayammum.* This is an Islamic ablution performed before prayers using earth in the absence of water.

TOWERING BLOOD

Negin Farhoud

When blood towers, heavenward
A half-closed gate is opened wide
So as to make up for drought,
Clouds drink blood, restoring it in the earth
And blood
The homesick, desiring blood
That filled the blank for each name
By its dripping, in search of its own face.
Then grasp the blood thrown out of blood
And take turn in the street's corpse
Towards the fine silk of her bosom
And bring as token
A sign of their companionship
To the masses:
Swearing
By the rising green,
As it runs to the edge of all winds,
Grooming the air
Swearing
By sound,
That has grown and glossed its childhood
By stone and case-shot,
Swearing
By the descended fair divine
Who decodes her own supreme name
And tears open the word "bright"
So as the lunar sisterhood
Burns the dissipating remains of night
Now, you,
The helping sisterly hands

CONT'D OVERLEAF

Whose fingertips
Deep in the ground
Are pointing at death
With dagger-like nails
Hang onto jasmine's fragrance and dethrone
The moon from its blazing heights
In that you are incandescent
In that your guidance incessant

CAPTIVATED BREATHS[1]
Parimah Avani

I resemble the dead
Enflamed
Rose to the invisible Danse Macabre of the living
In captivity
The cadaverous monument of an undead history
That snows, bitterly
Over memories and undelivered winter lasts forever and
Our fallen harden on our lips sewed up
And we ask "why alive?" with our smile
Gone with the wind
The run-down mountains of icefall
We, fallen one behind another, as do the mountains
Like crisp of air!
Partridges, awake under the snow
A blizzard half-met
What a history of disgrace and the last breath of yours
A sigh
From poetry's chest in your absence amongst us
O brother, the hag writes in your blood!
Every single sigh dripping shame
A "dark dwarf" out of each blood drop
A long scroll in hand, standing at a dystopian
    podium and
Reciting a poem of a thousand toads
In a boiling pot of your words
Your gloomy dark ghost-meadow
Is the hope of us, the dead,
Breathe against this stormy dust
So gurgles the blood
And wounds arise
As rises that river
That can't reach the sea.

¹ This poem is a homage to the last days in the life of Baktash Abtin, whose real name was Mehdi Kazemi. Baktash was an Iranian poet, writer, documentary filmmaker, and also a key member of the board of editors and former secretary of the Iranian Writers' Association. He was imprisoned for "propaganda against the state" and "actions against national security". After the authorities refused to treat him for COVID-19, he died on 8 January 2022, aged forty-seven. His final resting place became a conflict zone between activists and the authorities. Some protesters were arrested and dragged out of the cemetery by the regime's undercover police. Baktash's death caused a great deal of public anger, as well as outrage from the international cultural community. This was one of the most shocking and widely reported crimes committed by the regime before the emergence of the Woman Life Freedom movement later the same year.

MY PEOPLE

Proshat Kalami

Author's note: Composed in Virginia during the winter of 2023.

My people, from here,
Good or bad,
But still my people,
Look!
Good or bad,
They are falling rings
Of a lock of my hair
Falling rings
That my searching eyes track
Good or bad,
They are my stories

Here and there
In every place,
In Paris,
Boston,
They are the rings
Falling from my face
Look!
Look as I lay my head on the pillow
They are the falling rings
Of a lock of my hair
Faces without you, without me
People are but my searching eyes

IN ANALYSIS
Raziyeh Aghajari

In analysis,
It's a head-running thrill,
The human vodka
Dance!

The continuity I undergo
Laughed at all the blood
Filtered through follicle
For one another, when caressing.

A strand would suffice
Positively within reach
In a chronicled time
Do sigh!
The five-folded bedfellows
Young and old
In a romantic hesitation upon silks

You will not commit any equilibrium
Soak-rolling in vodka
Descend onto me from top of the strand
To the subtle curve of skin joints
This is the least allowed limit of politics
Then do desire.

I'VE SHAVED MY HEAD
Rira Abbassi

I have shaved my head, my Lord
My Lord, I have shaved my head behind
   dead-ending doors
Gift me with light
A door halfway through a conversation
I vanish into thin air, as I get drenched
How enrapt I am, when far away
How entrapped, a door fallen on the ground
A smokeless fag-end between lips, a shaved head
   among all heads
Heads whose universal farce is but a strand of my hair
I walk
Free is the air
So are tears
Bereaved eyes, the same, everywhere free
A gliding cup falling into the depths of solitude
Bitter brown eyes as blank as the white on my cup
Eyes of no abode
At a far corner of a crowded café,
It's raining and raining
The hissing overcoats, briefcases, hats
Squeaky laughing chairs, jackets,
Footfalls,
The red in English bricks, forever unburnt
Half-opened umbrellas,
Raindrops falling down
from brick-faces.

STRAIGHT OFF
Robab Moheb

At once, the woman's hair against the wind
At once, the woman's hair the rain-making cloud
At once, the woman's hair a river whose every strand
Blows into crying horns buried long
  in a worn-out throat

***

Her hair
Straight off,
Gone with the wind
Her hair
Straight off,
Turned into rain clouds
Her hair
Straight off,
The river of many strands
Blowing clamour
In a throat,
Worn out by cries.

THE VEIN
Roja Chamankar

Loose hold on the wind
So that the blood comes to boiling
In locked winter veins
So that fire whirls
In time's frozen corpus
Loose hold on the wind
So that it revives in your long hair

Demand it to go
From among us, this dark
So that death trembles under our tapping feet
Topple down
You, leaden limit of mourn
And demand deep paradise
To turn azure
So that there be a salvation for torn body parts
Honouring the vein
We flew through impassable crossings

Demand it to go
From among us, the dark
So that the colourful rainbow cataract pours out
Over the stretched shoulders of the day
And love's pure parts
Hair wrapped around mountain waistline
To dance on history's weary mind
Honouring every fallen offspring, next to the heart
Honouring mothers' wisps of hair cut off
Over empty cradles
Loose hold on the wind

So that it revives in your long hair
Bitter
As grapes bleeding in mourning
As the bottomless heavens cheer
At tears' doorway
To breathe a blazing fire
Under winter's skin

Demand it to go
From among us, the dark
Drink us!
In glorifying tears of these very nights
Recite us!
At the heart of this very impenetrable
Voice you.
A matron bereaved by the departed
Of an untimely death
The matron of all pains and gains!
Bring the time
Into dance, across our shanks!
Grow the world in our depths!
As a tribute to those roots
We took away from your bones

TO LEARN

Rouhangiz Karachi

Author's note: Composed in Tehran in 2021.

I have learned
To cry my dreams, slowly
And imprison love
In the white of papers
As stormy gusts advance
And be a woman
In a room with no window
Other than imagination.

THE ROOM NEXT TO SLEEP
Roya Tafti

Next to the south
Next to drought
And the room next to sleep
Even power escaped the razors
A machine, provisionally set, faking its sleep
All about you is de-configured too
Standing before my eyes, naked
Dead with precision, since you haven't moved
And, with the tweezers I have, I'd remove the same
   purulent pimple still fresh as day one
   – luring it step by step
For years, I've been pressing it
To reach the rhythm of a dance, singular
One of a kind

A FEVERISH SICKLE IN SOME HAND
Saghi Ghahreman

Author's note: Composed on 29 May 2022.

Give me your head >[1]
Give me your head >
Give me your head >
Give me your head >

Give me my head

Give me your head >

Give me my head

Give me your head >

Give me my head

Give me your head > Give me my head
Give me my head give me my head
Give me my head give me your head >
Give me my head give me my head

Give me my head
Give me my head
Give me my head

Give me my head
Give me my head

Give me its head
Give me its head

Give me your head >
Give me your head >
Give me your head >

Give me my head

Give me your head >
Give me your head >

Give me my head
Head head head head

Give me your head >
Head head head head
Give me your head >

Head head head head
Give me my head

Give me its head
Give me its head

CONT'D OVERLEAF   193

Give me my head
Head
Head
Head
Head
Give me my head
Give me my head
HHHH

H H H H
H
Give me its head
H
H
@

[1] The word "head" in this poem is used to connote many ideas. Perhaps: a person in charge of something – or a dictator or leader; the upper part of a human body, containing the eyes, ears, nose and mouth – or the glans penis or glans clitoris; an emphasised line of words printed at the top of a newspaper article – or the key points of broadcast news…

A CITIZEN ABANDONING HAPPINESS
Saideh Keshavarzi

Arrived to wash off the bloody surface of the day
And remove nectars spattered on the forehead of mishap
Came to flesh out the opening void of the chest
And to pronounce the corpse ready

I drew death near me hard
And its oak hands of five-fold paws around my neck
Letting petals of blister and blood in my canvas shoes
I drew death near me hard
A couple of buckshots neighing
A little emerald refined in my hollow life

You, died in the intervals of doubtful seasons
I took you in like thick smoke in my mucus
When you were no more in your bony face
As your lips; moistened life was decomposing
    to mortalise the form of a kiss
How your corpse thickened the soil?
How you died in Dar-ol-Rahmah cemetery while flying
    the cranes and swans off the collar?[1]
How did you manage, buried there, to project light
    from your throat onto the lunisolar years?
And you'd say, "Never to recover throughout life…"[2]
And your lifespan all burnt out?
And a row of brief nebulas in the cross-pathed sky
I kiss the future on its skullcap
And the Grand Name of tears,[3] known as Dry River[4]
Throbbing out of the nightly cry of slug and syringe
I spoke of collapsing
Of a few incidents happening in memories

CONT'D OVERLEAF   195

I spoke of collapsing
And a flood was barging in from the east side of Shiraz

Was the woman who'd swallow muddy waters
    as bread and salt
And would kiss the blood-shedding forehead
    of catastrophe in rosy waters[5]
Was she a citizen abandoning happiness?
Was that woman leaping from Safa Bridge[6]
To crush her living dreams on a stony bedrock
A woman commuting between home and streets
    in slug and lead
To descend upon her private grave
A woman flashing a pair of melancholic forearms
And her life dismantling over cracks on a complex
    in Vahdat Passageway[7]
Someone whose dead crane-hanging corpse would
    normalise our threshold of fear
Was the one who'd perish unremittingly
    and in continuity
A citizen abandoning happiness?

I said, "What antique brilliance lying on a morgue bed
When they carry the ablution of this poeticised shred?
What antique brilliance lying on a morgue bed
When will I recognise the beloved and death?"
I said, "What antique brilliance lying on a morgue bed
When will it be the time for me to acknowledge
    the fallen of Shiraz?"

[1] Dar-ol-Rahmah cemetery is located in Shiraz, central Iran.

[2] An allusion to the opening line of a sonnet by the prominent classical poet Sadi: "Never to recover throughout life from this crapulent after-drink / As I loved you before there was any me to think."

[3] This alludes to the Quranic version of Solomon the prophet and the grand divine code engraved on his royal ring. This code helped Solomon gain dominance over fairy creatures and suchlike.

[4] A dried-out river in Shiraz, known by the same name.

[5] In Farsi there is wordplay here with the syrupy nectar that is traditionally extracted in Iran – which in English is translated as rosewater. Hence, similar wordplay in English would change "rosewater" to "rosy waters".

[6] A bridge over the River Drey – the river previously mentioned in this poem.

[7] The Vahdat Passageway, or Kouy-eh Vahdat, is a neighbourhood in Shiraz.

FROM HERAT SCHOOL TO TEHRAN[1]
Samiranik Norouzi

A witness I was
After the meadows,
And trees bitter-greened by brush strokes
Chained to a mountain
The one the painter coloured white
Fast-paced, with a string of horses,
The chariot, the rider
Sigh to sigh and breath after breath
We revived the breaths enchained
From Herat to Tabriz
We witnessed her enchained in Tehran
Her voice, welling up from the depths
With no mythic Zal, weaving a thread
   from a woman's hair[2]
Neither to enchain
Nor to hang with
But to reach her singing lips

In chains determined not to let us go
We packed off as runaways
And it was in Isfahan, that I was drawn
By the painter, with broken legs

Now I was but a limping deer
As prophesied in King Tahmasp, The Book of Kings,[3]
Running away from the vision of Zahhak, the snake-
   shouldered tyrant,[4] enchained by green rangers,
   pulling the arrow out of my left thigh
Not seeing I get suffocated by the memory
   of women enchained

From Herat to Tehran
I ache at every joint for fourteen centuries plus
   or something
With Táhirih streaming from my eyes.[5]

NOTES: FROM HERAT SCHOOL TO TEHRAN (previous pages)

[1] The subtext of this poem – mentioning Iran's cities alongside its tradition of miniature painting – draws a parallel between the scenic content of such paintings, and the traditionally patriarchal and socially oppressed conditions of women in these cities – from ancient times until today. Both in terms of the title and the content, this poem resembles an ekphrasis: a vivid poetic description of a painting. This can be detected in the descriptions of small mythical heroes, figures, and animals. All are elements of Iranian miniature painting, as depicted in Shah Tahmasp's version of the Iranian classic, the *Shahnameh* (The Book of Kings).

[2] In Farsi, Zal literally means an individual suffering from poliosis (a lack of melanin, leading to white hair). This is the name of a character in Ferdowsi's epic classic, the *Shahnameh*. Zal is an epic hero who meets a young princess, Roudabeh; she is the daughter of Shah Mehran. Zal and Roudabeh fall in love, but cannot openly meet. So Rudabeh lowers her tresses from her balcony. Zal climbs to her bedchamber, and their night of passion leads to the conception of Rostam, the key epic figure in Ferdowsi's *The Book of Kings*. However, as explained above, the poem references one of the miniature illustrations in Shah Tahmasp's version of the Shahnameh.

[3] *The Shahnameh* of Shah Tahmasp is a high point in the art of the Persian miniature.

[4] Zahhak "The Snake-Shoulder" is an evil king in Iranian ancient mythology. He has a pair of serpents growing out of his shoulders – the result of a curse that daily forces him to feed the serpents the brains of two young men. Zahhak is eventually dethroned and subjected to regicide by Kaveh, a common blacksmith. One of the famous scenes portrayed in the Shahnameh – as well as in Shah Tahmasp's illustrated version of this classic book – is the scene of Zahhak's demise.

[5] *Táhirih* (The Pure One) is the title of a poem by Fatimah Baraghani, an influential Iranian poet born in the early nineteenth century. In addition to her poetry and activism connected with women's civil and educational rights, she is also celebrated as the first woman to have removed her hijab in protest. She was secretly executed for her iconoclastic feminism.

TRANSIENT SYNOVITIS OF THE HIP[1]
Samira Yahyai

Author's note: Composed on 22 April 2022.

A body fallen
In sleep, over the tree of broken hours
Except Thursday.
Well-diggers and corpse hand in hand
Some scribbles and crossing-outs

Coming to expiration, on dated paper
Say, the seventh of May: "I went for a walk today."
"I saw my friend. She didn't recognise me."

I've thrown up on street corners glass after glass
Wanted amnesia to take over, jump, take a walk,
   clench fists, die
May morning prayers call never come
On dated paper, sunset rise
The devil leaves not
A serpent grows from the God's swollen gum
So we ask which day it is
And if it is still in place
The pond, harbour, or senses

Except Thursday, the rest of it, alone
The paths in the rooms, alone
Behind the kitchen table
Lying down and crawling
When moving bowels
Choking on water
And all the same, while taking a walk, the form of dying,
   none requires a given history.
Except Thursday,

When the corpse rises from the odour of decay,
  comes to light, and draws near
Exposes burn-marks before the eyes
Drawing its knife and fork out of the skin
Asking to be tasted…
Unrest is salty
And even saltier in chest-crawl
The room salty, the dark, even saltier
No more than a dated ghost
That was you, crawling, snaked, descending away
Through the staircase and claws felt uneasy.

<hr />

[1] Medical jargon for inflammation in the hips.

THE GIRLO
Sara Afzali

The little girl was herself.
She was sitting on the steps of the shop below
    the crossroad, and
As soon as I looked at her, Banan's voice rang
    in my head.[1]
It was God… sitting on the stairs to remind me:
"Unaware of us…
She pulls my hand…"[2]

The hand has no sound.
It has lines like the desert road,
It reaches to the aqueduct…
That we go down to bring water, we get watered.
Suddenly we remember we left our voice up.

Raise your voice… Raise your hands…

God is in your hand, is sitting on the stairs…
    has gone to the aqueduct, to be watered in full.

To be watered in full, the little girl.

[1] Gholam-Hossein Banan (1911–86) is one of Iran's most beloved musicians and singers.

[2] The lines "Unaware of us… She pulls my hand…" are taken from the lyrics of a well-known song by Banan.

THE BLADE
Sara Khalili Jahromi

Every morning
Optimistic eyes
Carry the burning plate of the sun on their shoulder
Dragging it by force
And throw it into night's valley
I should leave these eyes be with their dull effort
Need to escape through the window and this
   fear-bringing sky pouring into the room
And whisper asking:
Is there anybody
To decapitate the red and dark serpents intertwined
with my body tissue?

You, my land of birth whose summer's finesse
Is seduction to every urban tree
Brewing nectar in female palm throats
And crowns you with lemons of gold
You, my land of birth whose thirsty earth I burnt
As I sobbed the most inflamed tears over you
And burnt your chest
As I left my dearest to you
You, the warm land
Hand me the blade of sunlight
You, and of a winter night
The moment moonlight shone in vain
And he was forcing his frozen words into my ears
   one by one
And blood had soaked the pillow
The moment that tears, a titanic dripping tongue,
   licking my naked body

CONT'D OVERLEAF   207

The moment the bird made no return and my shoulders
    covered in rust
You, the night even date-burning south summer
    wouldn't warm you up
Hand me your blade of cold

You the long street stretched in all ways
The uninterrupted memory of this insane century
Summon the owners of all those nails
That chronicled on your thighs
Summon the wearers of shirts unworn
Left behind in your arms
Summon the ones with sliced tongues
Who kissed you, one another, and the burning fire
You the eternal mourner
The weeper over the death of fragile saplings
You sheltered in your deep wounds
Hand me the blade of your rage

You the inflated silence
When acid and leprosy and worm and inflection
Chewed up your lips, leaving a figure of smile behind
When you were decapitated with one head in the north
And with the other in the south
And your fertile womb, in the capital
Advertised on massive municipal billboards
When you were receiving your share of the oil wells
And setting yourself on fire
Perhaps you would warm up, perhaps
Hand me the blade of your south
And yet you
You, the affected by natural born banishment
You, the local of nowhere other than
A pair of remote hands rotting under the ground
You, fed up with ways they take you in never to return
You, departure-aware despite what has grown out of
both your shoulders

And the laughter storm of migratory birds
Hand me the sad velvet of your solitude
So that one night, as moonlight shines in vain
Spread it at the window pane
And make them die on its soft plane
A pair of hunchbacked eyes
And all serpents intertwined with my body tissue.

DREAMS[1]
Sepideh Jodeyri

Engulfed by dreams, as if
The kiss I give,
A tad loftier,
A smidgen more startled.

And words devoid of edge,
The chasm they etch
Between the zenith of decay
And my insignificance, within weary nerves,
It's all but a whisper,
It's all but a whisper.

I morph into the silhouette of a condition,
The form of days only transpired,
I take the shape of the rice you've consumed,
I evolve into the finest grain in the world,
It's all but a whisper,
It's all but a whisper.

Only slumber has been your companion,
Nothing is birthed from sleep,
Only sleep takes your place in the cradle,
And love, jostles its vast dunes,
Next to every portal, a day,
A day trimmed from my futility,
Succumbs to the abyss of profound musings.

Let me tenderise my nerves, one granule at a time,
And leave them resting in that exquisite locus.
A nerve devoid of yearning for another

Takes the guise of a one-day demise,
Or perhaps twelve,
Who can say?
It's all but a whisper,
It's all but a whisper.

To one who sees sleep as the quarry of fleeting moments,
My kisses have moistened his lips,
Or rendered them chattier, all of it.
Some entity raises and strikes the fortune resting
    upon our crown,
A tad loftier,
A smidgen more startled.

Cats won't forsake an ignorant tutor,
Exuberance croons in their serendipity,
Let those who remain blind to this be blinded!
Doubt must be absolved, from whichever flank you can,
Reverts to the cats someday,
These hands that act but once a week.

I must wear down my forms,
I must tether my hands to beds known by Eros,
And lose myself in the act.
So that my sleep absconds,
So that my sleep does abscond,
That sleep, isn't worth a single farthing.
Night, has discovered a grander facet of itself,
Be crafted for the stroll,
Traverse the terrain of thrill,
Through my rigid thrill,
A tad loftier,
A smidgen more startled.

CONT'D OVERLEAF

This entity that is absolute or not,
Offers no echo of love,
Embrace me, my hand is in the throes of starvation,
And I evolve into the finest grain in the world.
It's all but a whisper,
It's all but a whisper.

[1] Translated from the Farsi, by Payam Hassanzadeh.

IMPREGNATED
Sepideh Kouti

I was impregnated
By musical unknowns
Notes oft-played

Much later,
My child
Had turned into
My mother,
Sub-lunar
Wrinkled hands
With stories far-fetched

A woman's tale
Lacking the know-how
For love letters,
That estranged music
Whirling in the wind

Her child turned into
Her mother
And rock,
Into her father,
As the river,
That into her brother
Forgetting her womanhood
Running free
With hair stretched long
To knee caps
Enflamed by burning fires
Till dawn

CONT'D OVERLEAF

Running
To converse
With the earth
Fire
Wind
That new-born fig tree
Fashioning words
By dewy letters
Hanging from the branches
Sunray
Thrown into the moss.

As she ended her talk
She fell asleep
Thickened the forest,
Steady rain
And her mother-child
Caressing her
For years, in sleep
By the form of words
Shed from her dreams
She was reminded of
Being a woman.

WHATEVER I LOOK AT
Shahin Mansouri

Whatever I look at
Whirls so much
That vortex goes vertiginous
The earth rounded up in my fist
Now that its body disseminates sins
Its rumbling, ever-higher
In the presence of streets and avenues
Calling the wind to testify
As it takes away
This nine-year-old girl's scarf!

SOMETIMES[1]
Sheida Mohammadi

Sometimes, I think of death
But sometimes,
Only
As wonder glows in your eyes
And paralysis runs across my veins
And suddenly, then
Death
Stares at your eyes
Looking back at it, in awe

"So fasten'd in her arms Adonis lies"[2]
And I, all in outcry, plucking unpluckable nerves
"Which bred more beauty in his angry eyes"
And stifled all stifling in my head to pull all strings

"For to a pretty ear she tunes her tale;"
Of the deafening silence in capillaries
Creeping slow, under my bloated skin
Of "crimson shame and anger ashy-pale;"

And I then
Wanting yet failing
To burst into outcry
And you are still afloat
In death's glassy eyes
You,
Mohammad,
Mohammad Hosseini
I only

And only
Sometimes, I think of death
As it and solitude hold hands
And warmly presses the blue veins on your hand
To the point where music is set off
And you, executed.
Sometimes, I think of the solitude
Who signed your death certificate
Sometimes, amidst sobbing,
I think of the azure lines on your hands
Of the hour when Death stared at them
Without having succeeded
In stealing the glow in your eyes away
O, Mohammad Mr
Mohammad Hosseini
Sometimes, I think of your long neck
Held between your hands
As if a pendulum over Tehran's roof
Of that captivating gaze
Kept staring at morning's awe
In Evin's paralysed nerves.[3]

O, Mohammad
Mohammad Hosseini
Sometimes, that is always, I think of you
Of how darling you were to the desert
Of your shoulders at poultry farm[4]
And of a basement going forty-four steps deep
To be welcomed by the slaughter-house dark
Of your teeth grinding silence
And of your executioner, abominably invoking God,
And of the black of the guardians of the divine army
Yes, Mohammad,
At bottomless nights of the names
Move from Abtin to Mahsa, and from Nika to
Mehrshad, and from Khodanour to you[5]

CONT'D OVERLEAF

And my sobbing stutters
As I cry you out
Sometimes, I think of death
Those "sometimes" that are "forever" to you.

FOR MAHSA AMINI
Shirin Razaviyan

Your hair
Sings freedom green
And the words of a poem turning into a cry
    in its own throat
Your body covered in blood
Will turn into a time-honoured pomegranate tree
That will tell the tale of dry-season spoil
To every traveller in thirst
You have rooted around
In that plagued soil
The innocence in your gaze, perhaps, the harbinger
    of liberation to thousands
When silk headscarves
Are set on fire
And long strands of hair
Dark and red and gold
Meet widening scissors[1]

Long live Woman
Long live Life
Long live Freedom
Long live me!

[1] This alludes to the Iranian feminist act of cutting part or all of one's hair as a form of protest. The countless repetitions of this gesture during the Woman Life Freedom demonstrations led to its imitation by other women worldwide. It is less well-known that, in ancient Iran, old women often cut their hair when mourning the death of loved ones, especially those who died in their youth. The gesture is described in Iranian classical literature, especially in Ferdowsi's *The Book of Kings*.

ARE YOU ASLEEP?
Shouka Hosseini

It is moonlit, the fiery heap of hair
Of each strand of it, gold falls on the ground
Each strand, turning into a hand, exposed to fire

Declaim!
Declaim
In the name of
The God of Woman
Of Life
Of Freedom

Fire sets maidenhair's ordeal ablaze[1]
The palm is moaning against dancing
    luminescent deities
Declaim
In the name of hair
These very bundles of gold
Golden framing hair
This very noose around the necks
These very throats freed, but from voice
These death-blown maidenhairs

Are you asleep?
Of each and every mantle strands
Fall the perishing young
On the earth, a sleep-rebound
The earth over-burdened by all the young inhumed

Gaze into the orient,
Where sets the sun
Where the monarchs
Are in search of executionable necks
Are you asleep?
Take your nose off the memories
That migratory birds share
Step upon this earth
Where we plant gold
Our offspring, ad infinitum,
Will find on it, one day
The treasure of now.

[1] "Maidenhair's ordeal" comes from the Farsi word *Siyavoushan*,
a cascading fern that is said to look like women's hair. In English, it
is known as Venus hair fern. Siyavoushan also refers to the mythical
figure *Siyavoush*, who was lauded in Ferdowsi's eponymous epic, *The
Book of Kings*. Siyavoush was wrongly accused by his adversaries, and
executed. He is still venerated in parts of Iran as a symbol of wronged
youth and unjust vengeance. Ferdowsi, born in 940, is considered one
of the most important writers in the history of world literature.

HER THROAT OVERRUN BY THE STREET
Soheila Mirzai

Author's note: Composed on 29 January 2023.

Dance me to fire
The flair of my hair, a flare
In my throat, fire in square
Cedars dancing in the street

A distant dream, shattered
Piles of street
I turned into blood, like a red fish
Only to be buried
I turn into blood
So they be buried.
I turn into a blood
On the wall, growing thick.

Venom is what mothers taste
Scaffold, cemeteries, lay in waste.

– Was she desensitised?
– They burnt her dream, before her eyes!

Let your hair be grown into a noose

– How will they map apart, the neck from the throat?

But now, love is put to another affair
But now, love is put to another affair
My kisses
My kisses in search of your neck
My songs, enamoured
For you, my splendid combatant!

THE OPENING CHAPTER

Solmaz Naraghi

Author's note: Composed in the spring of 2009.

In the name of Hurmozd, the merciful[1]

The benevolent giver

In the name of first-person narrators
The dark disobedient words
In the name of Damascus Drought[2]
Under the butchering sun
In the name of the warning phrase
Of crippling agonies, beyond repair
In the name of homo loquens,[3]
The agonised
Forlorn
Expressing beast
In the name of citizens insured
The formless impoverished stains
In the name of damned be the devil by God!
In the name of damned be the devil by God!

In the name of Hurmozd, the merciful

The benevolent giver

NOTES: THE OPENING CHAPTER (previous page)

[1] Hurmozd (God of Light) refers to the highest and most frequently invoked divine entity in Zoroastrianism: a pre-Islamic Iranian religion. The key opening prayer line: "In the name of Hurmozd, the merciful, the bountiful" commemorates this divine figure.

[2] This is an allusion to Saadi Shirazi's classical verse book, *Bustan* (The Orchard), completed in 1257. Bustan narrates the story of a drought-striken Damascus – a drought so severe that lovers were said to have "abandoned their love".

[3] "Speaking man." Homo loquens is a Latin term that posits that speech is the most distinctive aspect of human behaviour. Language evolved as primarily vocal, but it is also deeply entwined with non-vocal expression (writing and reading).

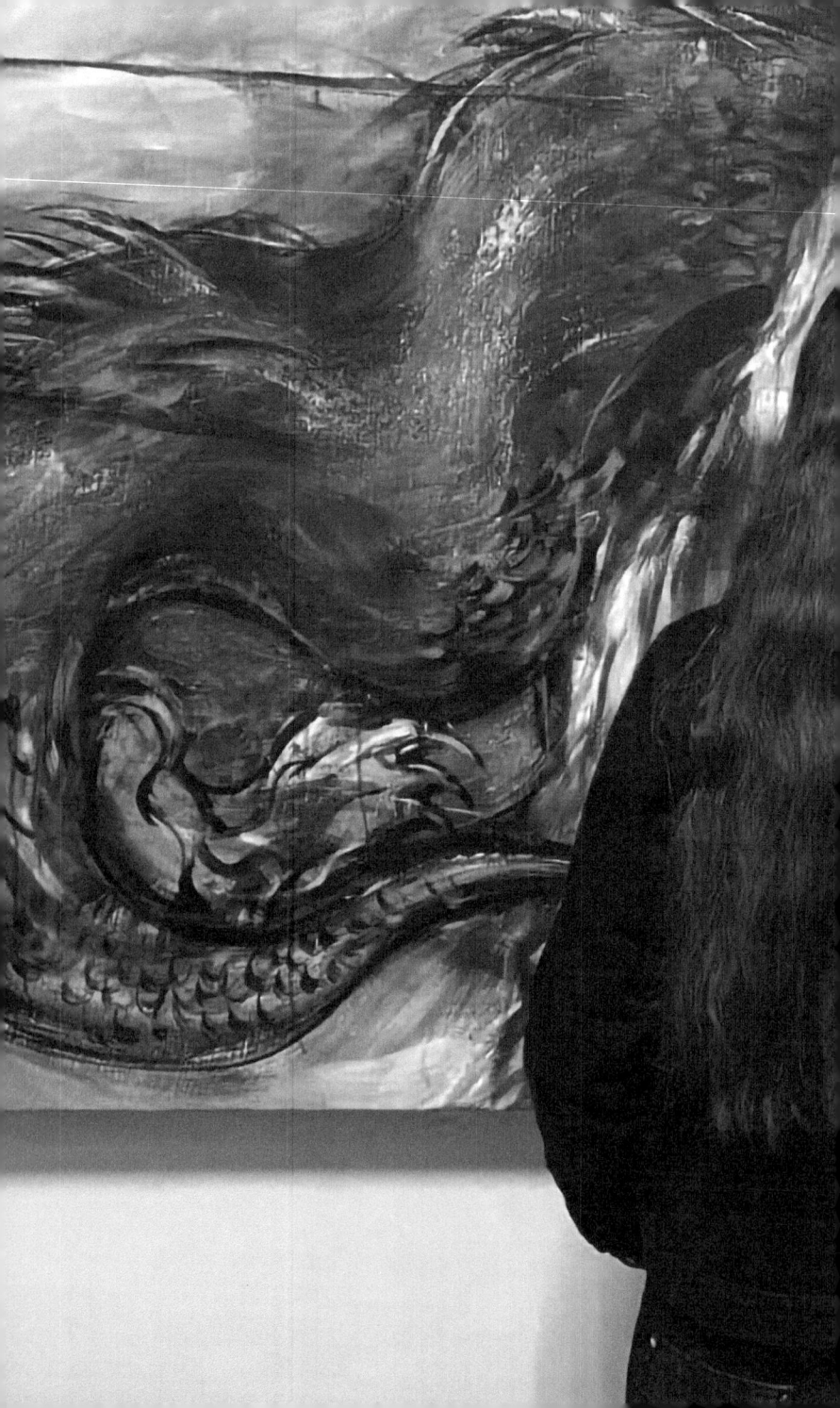

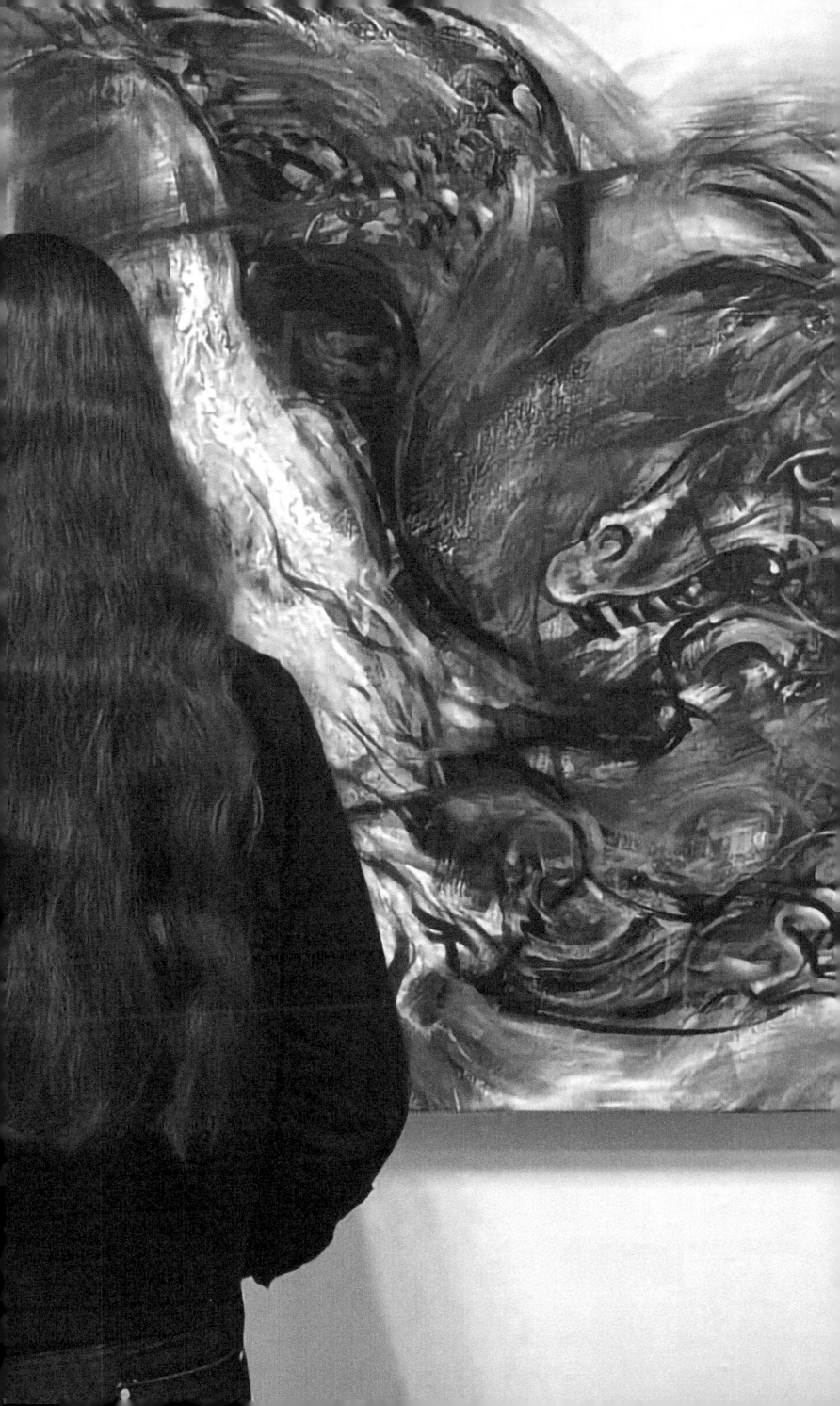

COMBING YOUR HAIR
Somayyeh Amini Rad

Comb your hair to nudeness
Comb sumac-azure summits
These goddesses playing strings in frothed jade.

Draw on water for clear conduct
Lay hands on locks cut from
Knead
Hair locks cut away from the waves
And of water, adopt the dress of thin fragrance
Adopt and approach a hand to lips
And to the rapid gasping humidity.

You, the colourless on the waves!
And your dress, gone with the wind
Which sea is it that you face?

In a windy cool;
Whistling undyingly
In a five-fold Canopus
Of the stars on your skirt
On shell-sides
A pearl surrendering itself
To itself
Cloaking itself in its beauty
In its rounded solitude

You, the woman, born
From and for the woman
You, the plural, loosened away from shell's sacrosanct
You with this mouth, nest for seagulls
In the constant white sand spray
As a crystalline music of the sea.

Coming from
The tinselled waves of mirage
Your presence, immersion
In shell moist
Brought from
The pentagonal scaly shores!

DEAD ON ONE'S OWN SOIL
Sofia Ahankoub

Dead on one's own soil
I mowed
Facing the moon
Where triumphant herds perished
So that wilderness's frequency
Gone astray in the trepidation of your coming
I was neighing a detailed sorrow
That other than that very liberating night
I sobbed throughout the year
And realised
"Growing separate but ever-prudent between us"[1]
Slid away word-free through your executing hands
In preparation of that graveless home
When young, I'd abandon the voice
When young, the sky would fall

In the summons of my chest
That pitted wishbone
The wishbone gone pale
Somewhere I could have been born a deer
On the verge of happening not
A gazelle, elsewhere, and in tears
With blushing fountains
To those others
To those ensuing me
To those speaking of you and
Of cold headwater
Stirring your history
I
Stone blood

In the moment of jest
With siding horns

– There where death was always above life –

And now, recite an agony of lined-up blood
A witness of wall and skin
With the same name
Left un-uttered in your mouth
In remaining body parts
In farmlands of wheat and flower planes
The silhouette of fancy in an accelerating twig
And what befalls you uninterruptedly
Where is a mourner to sing elegiacally for us,
Of a thousand words all summoned,
    though unexpressed?
Someone whose profile is doubled
The mediator of the dead and the earth
Speaking a new language.

[1] A line quoted from the prominent Iranian neoclassical poet,
Simin Behbahani (1927–2014).

APOSTROPHE (abridged)
Tayyebeh Shanbehzadeh

Author's note: Composed in March 2023.

...Hail to the bleeding lives of the rain
In the aftermath of a boot and gun downpour
Hail to those canes that tore our hearts apart
Over freedom's bright wings
On the reddened floor of the sky
Hail to the conglomerated clouds of downfall at noon
To the multitude collapsing sadness
To bruise's nest
Hail to the wretchedness
To decline
To Karoun riverbank as it gave back our corpses.[1]
Hail to sling bullets sitting on our chests
To the grudge of a hanging noose
   around our radiant daybreak
Do you hear, Leila?[2]
You are but all mother to sorrow
Call on!
We're standing, facing the wasted wind and Karoun
In purple veins of valleys and in graveyards
Pressed in our crumpled chests
Do cry
In a single-standing voice:

"Hail... hail
Hail to hearts shattered by mourning
To rumbling lives
To a plant smiling faintly at fresh young blood
Hail to hearts torn apart
To streets gone cold
To eyes blown out[3]

To tulips upside-down
To fire
To nests of wounds
To tombstones
To motherland's heart split open against windy banners
To the lives collapsed on asphalt
To the blood-soaking moonlight on the street
It's time for the two of us, Leila, to briefly cry
The whole of Karoun, in our heart,
Must well out through our eyes
And flow across the inflated arteries of the earth
To flatten the craggy land
To the blood clogged in our slumber
All these wretched mourning black
In all these Socratic months of hemlock in our spine
Let us briefly cry, Leila, over the wardrobes
Over the clothes with owners departed
You are all mother to sorrow
Restless at night
You caress the fair visage of codes on walls as you
wander about
Every night,
You go to the mountains
To rivers
Graveyards
And plant a flower
Honouring every single dove, they killed and buried
You garden nocturnal doves, Leila
Let us briefly cry."

NOTES: APOSTROPHE (previous pages)

[1] Almost certainly refers to the case of Donya Farhadi, a young female student who participated in protests against the regime – before disappearing. Her body was later found in Karoun River, in her home town of Ahwaz in southwest Iran. She had been shot to death.

[2] This most probably alludes to a one of the "Justice-seeking Mothers", who lost a child in the course of the bloody crackdowns against Woman Life Freedom demonstrators.

[3] A reference to the widespread use of powerful shotguns favoured by the regime's oppressive forces. They are authorised to "systematically and deliberately" (Iran's Human Rights Organisation reports) target protesters' eyes during Woman Life Freedom demonstrations. Numerous young protesters who lost an eye as a result of this brutal measure later revealed their identities on social media and continued the struggle by other means. Some human rights reports speak of at least five hundred recorded cases of eyesight being destroyed in this way.

FERNAND LÉGER[1]
Zeynab Saber

Fernand Léger envisioned women round-shaped
Breasts, heads, bellies and arms all rounded up
My husband
Envisions me as suggestion box
He says one day

– Being absent-minded and all –

I will set the house on fire
I'm patient
And calm
And behind my ear
There is a city
That I leave everything to
Mortgage papers
Telephone bills and promotion application forms
With it, my mixed-up hormones
And having to dry the dishes
I crawl under a blanket

– With all my round shapes –

And think to myself
One day I should travel to Africa…

[1] Fernand Léger (1881–1955) was a French artist, sculptor, and filmmaker. He created a personal form of cubism that he gradually modified into a more figurative, populist style – so much so that he is often considered the first pop artist.

DANCING ON THE LASH

Zobeydeh Hosseini

Author's dedication: To Mahsa, Nika, Hananeh, and all the precious
lives lost during the Woman Life Freedom protests.

I'm dancing on the lash
And on the wall of letters
We set ourselves to engrave, wound, and scream,
Can I join in rending the night?
Or am I capable of death's double
And of crushing pain?

Mahsa, for me, an August of blood crushed
   between teeth[1]
Teeth of rage rending the lips
And for me, Nika, the flood of blood in my body
   torn apart[2]

And I recorded the cries:
The abducted young trees
They plucked young trees
And their roots walked off in the street
Itself gone walking
They plucked tongues
Yet bleeding words have walked away

Write on dust's forehead as such:
The heart's engagement on a skin gone blue
Disintegration on a netted plane
As if dismantling a body to force confession
Standing, in shock
Looking at your own pieces torn
And a grand revelation
As if an emancipatory blade
Assimilated into your remains
Your hair set free
Your roots all over the street

Zobeydeh Hosseini's dedication; they are:

Mahsa Amini: her death was the catalyst for the Woman Life Freedom protest movement. Mahsa was twenty-two years old when she was killed in police custody in Tehran on 16 September 2022, during a family trip to Iran's capital city.

Nika Shakarami: a sixteen-year-old who disappeared in Tehran on 20 September 2022, during the protests that followed the murder of Mahsa Amini. Nika's family was informed of her death – which has been blamed on Iran's security forces – ten days later. After Nika was identified by her family, they planned to bury her in Khorramabad, in the west of the country. But her body was allegedly stolen by Iranian authorities and instead buried in tiny Hayat'ol Gheyb, some forty kilometres away. This was reportedly carried out to exercise leverage over the family, and to avoid a funeral procession in a larger town, which could lead to further protests. Nika's brutal murder caused both national and international outrage, and nearly two years later, her family (as are many other victims' families) is under immense security pressure.

Hananeh Kia: was shot and fatally wounded by Iranian Revolutionary Guard forces on 21 September 2022. She was twenty-three years old. Like Nika Shakarami, Hananeh was shot during a Woman Life Freedom demonstration – this time in Nowshahr, on Iran's north-central coast. When Hananeh was targeted, however, she was not participating in the protests, but returning home from the dentist. When rushed to hospital, it is reported that she cried out to nurses, "Please, don't let me die… My wedding is in two weeks."

ACKNOWLEDGEMENTS

The editors would like to express their gratitude to
all those who sent us poems. Mainly owing to space
constraints, we were unable to include a representative
poem by some of the poets who responded to our call.

Special thanks to the unknown photographers whose
portraits of their friends, family members or partners
appear in *Hairan*: